Dutch Oven

A Cook Book
of coveted traditional recipes
from
the kitchens of Lunenburg

NIMBUS PUBLISHING LIMITED

Nimbus Publishing Limited
PO Box 9166
Halifax, NS   B3K 5M8
(902) 455-4286

Printed and bound in Canada

National Library of Canada Cataloguing in Publication Data
Main entry under title:
Dutch oven: a cook book of coveted traditional
recipes from the kitchens of Lunenburg

ISBN 0-921054-23-8
Previously published: Lunenburg, Nova Scotia: Progress-Enterprise, 1953.

1. Cookery, Canadian—Nova Scotia style. 2. Cookery—Nova Scotia—
Lunenburg. I. Lunenburg Hospital Society, Ladies Auxiliary

TX715.D88   1989   641.59716'23   C89-098528-6

Dutch Oven

A Cook Book
of coveted traditional recipes
from
the kitchens of Lunenburg

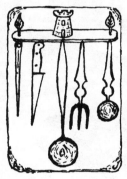

compiled by
The Ladies Auxiliary
of
The Lunenburg Hospital Society
1953

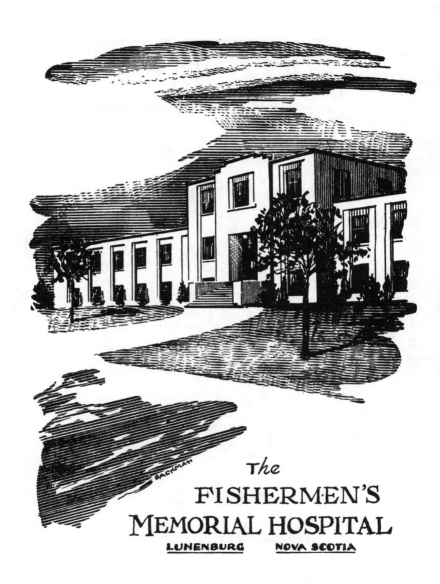

The
FISHERMEN'S
MEMORIAL HOSPITAL
LUNENBURG   NOVA SCOTIA

INTRODUCTION

This subject of eating can be a controversial one, and probably sooner or later we have to make up our minds as to whether we live to eat or eat to live.

It probably would have been more to the point if some eminent doctor or dietitian had been asked to write this preface rather than one that happens to be in the mayor's chair at the time of the town's reaching its two hundredth anniversary. Such an authority in all probability would have told you that our eating habits are essentially wrong and that we indulge in far too many carbohydrates and not enough proteins and green vegetables.

The receipts that follow will without doubt entice the appetite and prove the theory that for the most part we live to eat, thus further proving that, as doctors tell us, more people die from overeating than from overdrinking.

You are going to find some recipes that have been handed down from one generation to another during the last two hundred years. Among these will be barley bread, chicken noodle soup, and several ways to cook dry-salt codfish, all delectable dishes fit for the gods. I highly recommend them.

I wish to congratulate the members of the Ladies' Auxiliary of the Lunenburg Hospital Society for their initiative in getting out this cook book to help commemorate our Bicentennial and, at the same time, just a closing word of advice:- watch your waistlines.

J. Homer Zwicker
Mayor of Lunenburg 1953

ROUS'S BROOK
The Landing Place of the German Settlers
June 7, 1753.

Minnie C. Hewitt

Two hundred years ago a brave band of men and women landed on these shores of Lunenburg and began a new life. This group came from parts of Germany subject to the British Crown after the accession of George I, Elector of Hanover. Our present gracious Queen, Elizabeth II, is the ninth sovereign direct in line since George I.

Those early settlers were an industrious people, accustomed to reaping harvests from the land. In the new country, they and their successors became famous reaping harvests from the sea. Although through the years the people of Lunenburg changed completely their mode of living, yet they managed to preserve much of the culture and traits of their forefathers. Lunenburgers are well known for their hospitality, their distinctive dialect, their persevering nature, their love of music and their pride in community achievement. They still practise many of the old customs and cook many of the old dishes.

Today, as the townsfolk celebrate the 200th Anniversary of the founding of their town and the Coronation of their Queen, they are working together to "launch" their latest community effort, The Fisherman's Memorial Hospital. It is in support of this project and with the hope of doing a small service in preserving the recipes of some of the traditional Lunenburg dishes, that this cook book is published by the Ladies' Auxiliary of the Lunenburg Hospital Society.

5

– Acknowledgements –

The publishing of "Dutch Oven" is a project of which we long had dreamed but only in this Bicentennial year did we muster enough courage to implement it.

We owe a debt of gratitude to Mr. Philip Backman for his inimitable full page illustrations and for his advice and encouragement.

To our one and only Earl Bailly we tender our sincere thanks for his illustration of the front cover.

To Miss Minnie Hewitt, School Mistress Emeritus, Extraordinary, we say bravo and many thanks for the frontispiece and other contributions.

Our Cook Book Committee
Mrs. Andrew Eisenhauer, Convenor
Mrs. Aubrey Tupper,
Mrs. Thomas Himmelman
Mrs. Malcolm Smith

require special mention. Without their stalwart efforts and dauntless enthusiasm this book would still be a mere dream.

The cooperation of the whole community was necessary to compile this book, and its sponsors, The Ladies' Auxiliary received full cooperation as in all previous projects

We wish also to express our sincere thanks to our publisher Mr. D. J Bourque of the Progress-Enterprise for his patience and courtesy.

Catharine M. Creighton
President – Ladies' Auxiliary

6

Illustrations

7

Contents

Old LUNENBURG dishes

Dutch Mess or House Bankin
Salt Cod & Potatoes

½ lb salt dry cod
6 large potatoes
2 oz salt pork
Butter size of egg
2 onions
1 tbsp. vinegar
2 or 3 tbsp. cream

Tear cod in small pieces. Wash thoroughly and soak in cold water 3 or 4 hours. Peel potatoes and cut in six or eight strips. Remove fish from water and cook potatoes in water in which fish has been soaked. When potatoes are half done add fish and cook until potatoes are tender. Drain. Place on platter and sprinkle with pepper. Dice pork small and fry until brown. Add onions cut on the round and fry until light brown. Add butter, vinegar and cream, let come to a boil and pour over fish and potatoes.

Fish Cakes

Mash while hot left over fish and potatoes make in patties. If too dry add an egg or extra butter. Fry in cirses and butter.

Lois J. Himmelman
(Mrs Thomas)

Tongues and Sounds

Wash tongues and sounds in several waters. Soak in cold water over night. Put them in a saucepan, cover with cold water and bring to boiling point. Let simmer for 15 to 20 mins. Then drain

Cut salt pork in small cubes and fry with minced onions until pork is crisp. Add pork scraps and onions to fish.

Mildred Walters
(Mrs Angus Walters)

FISH MARKET

11

Solomon Gundy.
(Salmagundi.)

2 salt herring
1 large onion
Vinegar to cover.

Clean herring thoroughly, remove skin, fillet and cut in 2 inch pieces. Soak in cold water for 5 hours, changing the water frequently. (or soak over night if desired) Drain. Heat vinegar add 1 tblsp sugar, little pepper and cool. Pour over onion and herring and let stand for a few hours

Lillie M Deal
(Mrs J. W. Deal)

NOVA SCOTIA
LUNENBURG
"Gundy" Area!
BEWARE!!

Lecture In Herring Safety — Prof. Solomon

Hodge Podge

A dinner of new vegetables.

Cut new string beans and carrots into pieces. Cover with boiling salted water. Add cut potatoes - Cook 15 minutes. Add shelled peas and cook until tender.

Broad beans, sugar peas, cauliflower cook separately and add to the platter of vegetables.

1 c. finely diced salt pork fried to a golden brown, add 1c. cream, 1c. liquid, a little chives, pepper or a dash of paprika. Boil up quickly, dribble over vegetables. (omit onion).

Evelyn V. B. Rikery
(Mrs. C.D.)

Kartoffelsuppe
(Potato Soup)

1 quart diced potatoes
2 quarts water.
1 large onion, sliced
2 tsp. salt
½ tsp. pepper
3 ounces sheer fat pork
6 tbsp. flour

Method: Cut pork in small cubes and fry until light brown. When slightly cool put in pot with potatoes, water and onion, and cook until potatoes are soft. Put flour in pan where pork was fried and brown it, stirring constantly. Add the browned flour to soup and stir until the flour is dissolved. Add seasonings and boil 1 minute. Serve a small dish of sauerkraut with each serving of soup.

Ada S. Hebb (Mrs. W. H.)

14

Kohl Cannon

- 1 head cabbage
- 5 slices turnip
- 5 medium size potatoes.
- 1/4 lb. butter
- salt and pepper

Cook cabbage and turnip for three quarters of an hour. Add sliced potatoes and cook. When cooked, drain and mash with butter, salt and pepper.

Phoebe V. Conrad.
(Mrs. R. D.)

Old Song About Sauerkraut.

Sauerkraut is bully
Sauerkraut is fine;
We ought to know it
For we eat it all the time.

Put the cabbage in a "bar'l,"
Stamp it with your feet,
When the juice begins to rise
The kraut is fit to eat.

Put it in a pot,
Set it on to "bile,"
Be sure to keep the cover on,
Or you'll smell it half a mile.

Minnie C. Hewitt   16

Sauerkraut

Sauerkraut is a traditional Lunenburg food, therefore there are various ways of preparing and serving it. Sauerkraut juice is a very appetizing and nutritious beverage, and sauerkraut apples (which are placed in the barrel when the kraut is being made and left there until they become soft and juicy) are a delicacy.

Boiled Sauerkraut

3 lbs. corned beef   ½ lb. grown through pork

4 lbs. sauerkraut

Put meat in pot with enough water to cover. Bring to a boil, then reduce heat and simmer for 1½ hours. Add sauerkraut and continue to cook for 1½ hours. Drain the kraut and serve with the meat and mashed potatoes. Fresh beef, loin of pork or spareribs may be used in preference to corned beef.

Baked Fresh Spareribs with Sauerkraut

4 lbs. spareribs — split in two

3 lbs. sauerkraut

Place spareribs in roaster and bake ½ hour in oven 350°F. Remove pan from oven, lift up spareribs and put sauerkraut underneath. Turn spareribs, placing them over the kraut and bake 1½ hours longer. Serve with creamed mashed potatoes

Joyce L. Tupper
(Mrs. J. A)

TURNIP KRAUT

B.A.J.

Cut turnip in $\frac{1}{4}$ inch slices, then cut each slice in $\frac{1}{4}$ inch strips (like noodles)

Cube about $\frac{1}{3}$ pound clear salt pork and fry out in large skillet.

Add turnip, $1\frac{1}{2}$ c. water $\frac{1}{3}$ c. vinegar, 2 tbsp sugar $\frac{1}{8}$ tsp pepper

Simmer 2 to 3 hours. Stir it occasionally and add a little water to help it from cooking dry. Watch it closely as it burns easily.

Lillian Mosher
(Mrs Stephen)

18

Kohl (Cole) Slaw

Fry out ½ lb clear pork which has
been cut in small cubes

I often use a piece of butter (size of egg)
crisco or bacon fat in place of pork
1 small head of cabbage
chopped very fine.
1 cup brown sugar
¾ cup vinegar
salt and pepper to taste,
cook for 1½ or 2 hours.

Jean Burno Smith
(Mrs Malcolm)

19

Cucumber Salad

Peel 3 medium sized cucumbers. Slice very
thin and cover with 1 tsp. salt. Press with heavy
weight for about 2 hrs. One small onion (cut fine)
may be added to the cucumbers before pressing. if
so desired. Then drain liquid off cucumbers.
Add 4 Tbsp. of cider vinegar
  ½ Cup white sugar
   ¼ tsp. pepper
  ¾ Cup thick sour cream
Mix well with the drained cucumbers.
Tastes differ - so more sugar and vinegar may be
added to suit the taste.
This recipe will serve 8-10.

Lettuce and Sour Cream Salad

Wash 1 bunch of leaf lettuce, and cut
in thick shreds with scissors.
Make a dressing of 3 Tbsp. of vinegar
  ½ Cup. sugar (scant)
  ½ Cup sour cream.
Mix well and pour over the lettuce.
Mix slightly. Here again more or less
sugar and vinegar may be added to
suit the individual taste

Catharine M. Creighton (Mrs. H. A.)

20

Barley Bread.

8 cups flour, (5 white and 3
barley if flour is dark.)
2 tablespoons brown sugar,
1 Tablespoon salt (scant.)
½ yeast cake, dissolved in
1 cup of warm water, and a
small piece of butter.
Mix to a soft dough, let rise
until light, then pour into pans
making two loaves, and let
rise again, until the pans
are level full, then bake ¾
of an hour, or when the bread
leaves the pans. Bake in a hot
oven 350° After they are baked
brush melted butter over the top.

Mary C. Oxner.

(mrs. S. W.)

21

LOAF CAKE

2 qts. flour

1½ tbsp salt

1½ pts warm water

¾ cup shortening

3 cup sugar

1½ lbs raisins

2 yeast cakes

pinch soda and nutmeg nd lemon

Rub sugar and shortening through flour. Mix to soft dough. Let rise over—night. Bake about 1 hour (at 350° for 15 minutes and then at 325.) On removing from oven brush top with following mixture: 2 tbsp. milk, 2 tsp sugar, few drops vanilla.

May Eisenhauer (Mrs. D. M.

22

Raised Doughnuts

1 cup milk	½ cup sugar
1 yeast cake	¼ cup melted butter
5 cups flour	½ tsp. salt
2 eggs	½ tsp. mace

Scald the milk and cool to lukewarm. Dissolve the yeast cake and add it to the milk and a sufficient amount of the flour to make a sponge. Allow this to rise until double in bulk. Then add the eggs, sugar, melted butter, salt and mace. Beat thoroughly and add enough flour to make a dough. Knead this until it is smooth and elastic and let it double in bulk. Roll out on a board into a sheet about ¾ inches thick. Cut into long strips about ¾ inches wide, twist, stretch and shape in figure eight. Let these stand on the board or in a pan until they are light and then fry in deep fat.

(Sufficient for 3 doz. doughnuts)

Laura A. Myra (Mrs. N.A.)

23

Old-Fashioned Molasses Cookies

2 cups Molasses
1 cup Shortening
1 tsp. Nutmeg
½ tsp Cloves
2 dessertspoons Cinnamon
2   "   Ginger
2   "   Soda

Mix: Put on stove and let boil one minute. Take off and beat until cool. Then add:

1 beaten egg
5 cups unsifted flour

Bake in 350° oven, ten to fifteen minutes.

BELLE BACKMAN MACK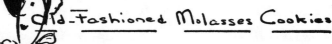
(Mrs S. E. Mack)

24

Pork Cake

Fat Pork	1 lb free of rind
Strong Coffee	1 pt.
Brown Sugar	1 cup
Molasses	1 cup
Eggs	2
Flour	5 ½ cups ½ cup to put over fruit
Soda	1 tsp.
Cloves	1 tsp
Cinnamon	1 tsp
Raisins	2 lbs. Seeded 1 lb. Seedless
Dates	1 lb.
Figs	If desired
Mixed Peel	½ lb.
Nuts	½ lb Almonds.

Weigh Pork free of rind, grind fine, then pour boiling hot coffee over it, and let stand a few minutes on stove Cool, Before adding any of the ingredients. Sift spices with flour and have fruit well floured. This makes 2 good sized cakes. Bake about 2 hrs.

Edie Tanner
(Mrs. Tracey)

25

Curd

Let skim milk stand until sour and thick. Put on stove and heat (stir occasionally) until curd starts to separate from whey. Do not let it get hot or curd will be hard and crumbly. Pour into a white cotton bag made with a draw-string and let hang to drain for several hours. Blend with sweet cream and a pinch of salt and serve with preserved fruit. Blend with sour cream and salt and serve as a cheese.

Ida E Himmelman
(Mrs L. A. H.)

26

Buttermilk Pie

1⅓ c. sugar
3 tbsp flour
3 c Buttermilk
3 eggs
2 tbsp butter

Beat egg yolks add to buttermilk, add flour and sugar and beat well. Fold in stiffly beaten egg whites. Pour into two unbaked pie shells. Dot with butter, bake until set.

Ethel F. Mosher
27 (Mrs Daniel)

Blueberry Grunt

1 qt blueberries
½ c water
½ c sugar or more to taste.

Boil berries, water, and sugar in a saucepan until there is plenty of juice.

Sift together 2 c flour, 2 tsp B.P. ½ tsp salt, and 1 tsp sugar. Cut in 1 tbsp butter with knife then add sufficient milk to make a soft dough like biscuit dough. Drop by tbsp over berries, cover closely, and cook for 15 min.

Beulah Thurlow
(Mrs James)

Sausage

20 lbs pork	4 tablespoons salt
15 lbs. good beef	2 tablespoons Allspice
1/4 lb. pepper	1 tablespoon summer
1/2 cup Coriander	savory

Grind pork and beef together, add spices, and mix thoroughly, put ingredients back in mill and roll on casings, fill sausage, cut in fifteen inch lengths, and hang up to cool for one hour.

Cook or fry sausage for ten minutes before eating. Sausage cooked with Sauer Kraut is good.

: Soak well 15 yds. of casings in warm water before using:

James Allen

29

Puddings

15 lbs. pork	3 qts. hot water
15 lbs. beef	4 tablespoons salt
1/4 lb. pepper	3 tablespoons summer
1 tsp. allspice	savory

Cook beef and pork together about 2 hours, let cool, take out bones. Grind meat, then spice, and mix well with water, then put meat in pudding filler, attach casings which have been cut in fifteen inch lengths, and tied with string, then fill, put five puddings on larger string in boiling water and cook 10 min. hang on pole to dry. Slice cold to eat or fry 10 min. on both sides.

: Soak well 15 yds. of casings in warm water before using:

James Allen

Beverages and Canapes

Christmas Cocktail.

4 c. cranberries.

4 c. water

Cook until very soft. Strain through cheesecloth.

Add ⅔ c. sugar

Heat and stir until sugar is all dissolved. Chill

Before serving, add equal quantities of ice-cold ginger ale, pineapple juice and orange juice.

Alice Adams.
(Mrs. E. C. Adams)

32

Raspberry Vinegar

Cover 4 quarts berries with vinegar and let stand 24 hours. Drain off liquid, squeeze out juice and measure the whole. Add an equal measure of sugar. Put in kettle and boil 20 minutes. Bottle, seal with Parawax and keep in dark place.

Rhubarb Punch

1 quart rhubarb
1 quart water
$\frac{1}{3}$ cup orange juice
4 tbsp. lemon juice
$1\frac{1}{2}$ cups sugar syrup
   (equal parts sugar and
               boiling water)
few grains salt
1 pint mineral water
      (or ginger ale)

Cut rhubarb in small pieces and cook in water until fruit is soft. Strain through cheesecloth. Add orange juice, lemon juice, syrup and salt. When ready to serve, pour over ice cubes in punch bowl, add mineral water and allow to get very cold. Makes 8 glasses or 24 punch glasses.

May Eisenhower
(Mrs. D. M.)

33

Punch

3 cups Sugar
1½ cups water
1 cup Tea Infusion
1 cup Strawberry or Raspberry
    Syrup
1 cup Grated Pineapple
½ cup Lime Juice
Juice 5 Lemons
Juice 5 Oranges

Make syrup by boiling sugar and water 10 minutes. Add tea infusion (2 tsp. Tea and 1¼ cups Boiling water). Add other ingredients and let stand 30 mins. Add ice water to make 2 gallons. Add 1 cup maraschino Cherries
    1 quart Gingerale
    Orange Slices
Serve in Punch Bowl with large piece of ice.   Serves 50.

Gladys B. Smith

Ginger Cordial

6 qts water   6 cups sugar
Dissolve sugar in 3 qts. boiling
water Then add 3 qts cold
water and ginger cordial
mixture while lukewarm
Caramelize 2 cups sugar to
tint the ginger cordial a
pale yellow
Pour into bottles and cork

Ginger Cordial Mixture
2 drams. Tr Capsicum
2 drams Tr. Ginger   } obtained
2 drams. Ess Lemon   from
1 dram. Tartaric Acid   Druggist.

A. Kinley

35

Tomato Juice Cocktail

1 can tomatoes

½ can tomato soup

½ can clam juice

1 cup water

1. medium onion

1 tbsp catsup

½ tsp celery salt

1½ tsp sugar

2 or 3 drops tabasco sauce

2 or 3 drops lea perrins sauce

Chop onion and boil a few minutes. Press tomato through sieve. Add juice of boiled onion and other ingredients. Mix well and chill.

Peggy R Leeland
(Mrs. J. A.)

36

French Chocolate

Grate 2½ 1-ounce squares unsweetened chocolate; add ½ cup water, and cook over low heat until thick, stirring constantly. Add ½ tsp. salt and ¾ cup sugar; continue cooking 4 minutes.

Fold in ½ cup heavy cream, whipped.

Store in refrigerator.

To serve, place 1 heaping tbsp in each cup and fill with hot milk; stir well.

Vive Le Chocolate Français!!

Libby Taylor
(Mrs. Robert Taylor)

Fish Canape Suggestions

Salt cod fish in strips.

Slices of smoked salmon or halibut
(flitch) on toast,

Squares of marinated herring (Solomon.
Gundy) on small slices of raw onion
set on a cracker or toast garnished with
a tiny pickled red pepper.

Sardines creamed with mayonnaise,
grated onion and lemon juice served
on melba toast.

Hot Tuna Canape:
Mix flaked tuna with mayonnaise or
salad dressing, add chopped stuffed
olives. Season with Worcestershire sauce.
Spread on toast strips, sprinkle with
grated American cheese. Place under
broiler unit or burner until cheese is
melted. Serve hot.

Salmon and Egg Canape:
Blend hard-cooked egg yolks flaked salmon
and mayonnaise or salad dressing to
smooth paste. Toast sliced bread squares
on one side. Spread salmon mixture
on untoasted side. Garnish with
chopped parsley and hard-cooked egg white

38

Anchovy curls or filets on toast fingers, edges dipped in mayonnaise and then sieved egg yolks, garnished with strips of pimento.

Tiny baking powder biscuits and tiny cream puff shells filled with lobster or any chopped fish mixture and serve hot.

Whole shrimp set on a small cracker which has been spread with tartar sauce colored green.

Potato chips topped with chopped lobster moistened with Russian dressing.

B. Jean Morrow
(Mrs. C. J.)

Pigs-in-Blankets.

For canapés slice small sausages in half lengthwise and roll in pastry and bake in hot oven till pastry is done. The rolls may be sliced in desired sizes before or after baking.

Prunes-in-Bacon

Soak prunes over night. Remove pits. Roll each in lean piece of bacon. Toast under broiler.

Angels on Horseback.

Salt oysters very lightly. Roll each in a strip of bacon and skewer with a toothpick. Grill or bake in hot oven till the oyster curls around the edges, and the bacon is crisp. Baste frequently with bacon fat.

Verna D. Smith
(Mrs. Russell G. Smith).

40

UNLOADING A SALT BANKER

41

Canapés

1.

Cornucopias

Roll salami or small bologna slices in cornucopias and fasten with a pick. Fill with white creamed cheese, flavored with horse radish.

2.

Wrapped Sweet Pickles

Wrap sweet pickles in fillets of smoked salmon or anchovy. Serve with a pick.

3.

Peanut Butter and Bacon

Spread prepared toast bed with crunchy peanut butter. Sprinkle with crumbled crisp bacon. Trim with minced parsley.

Toast beds may be square or rectangular.

1.   2.   Johanna Zuicker

Mushroom Tarts

3 tbsp butter
3 tbsp flour
1 can mushrooms
½ cup light cream
1 tsp. finely chopped onion
¼ cup chopped celery
salt and pepper
pinch paprika

Melt butter and flour, add juice from canned mushrooms and other ingredients, simmer for five minutes. Fill small pastry tart shells with hot mixture.

Cheese Squares

Blend equal quantities of cheese and butter and add mayonnaise to make a moist paste

Cut bread in ¾ inch slices and divide each slice into 4, making squares. If bread is not fresh moisten squares by dipping them in cream. Spread tops and sides with cheese mixture

Garnish with small pieces of bacon, dabs of marmalade or slices of olive. Place under broiler until lightly browned. Serve hot.

Peggy R. Sueland
(Mrs. J. A.)

43

Cocktail Sauce

½ cup catsup or Chili sauce
3 Tbsp. Lemon juice
Few drops Tabasco
¼ tsp. salt
½ cup finely chopped celery
2 tsp. Worcestershire sauce
Horseradish to taste

Mix all ingredients together and keep
in screw-top jar

Potato Chip Spread

1 can of condensed tomato soup
½ cup mazola salad oil
⅓ cup cider vinegar
1 tsp. Worcestershire sauce
2 tbsp. sugar
1 tsp. dry mustard
1 tsp. paprika
1 tsp. salt
Clove of garlic ⎫ optional
¼ cup cheese ⎭ optional

Measure ingredients into a jar
Cover tightly and shake well. Chill.

B. Jean Morrow
(Mrs. C. J.)

44

"Serve With After-Dinner Coffee"

Hot Cheese Puffs

Beat 2 egg whites until stiff.

Beat in: ½ tsp. baking powder
        ½ tsp. salt
        ¼ tsp. paprika

Fold in: ½ C. grated sharp cheese.

Heap on: 1½" rounds of prepared
           toast beds

Broil 5 minutes until delicately brown.

Caviar Toast Sandwiches

Put caviar in a shallow dish

Add: mayonnaise (1 tbsp.) until it is a
     creamy consistency

Add: juice of 1 lemon
     1 tsp. grated onion

Press together and cut in fingers.

Brown lightly and quickly under broiler.

Johanne Quickes

Boiled Coffee.

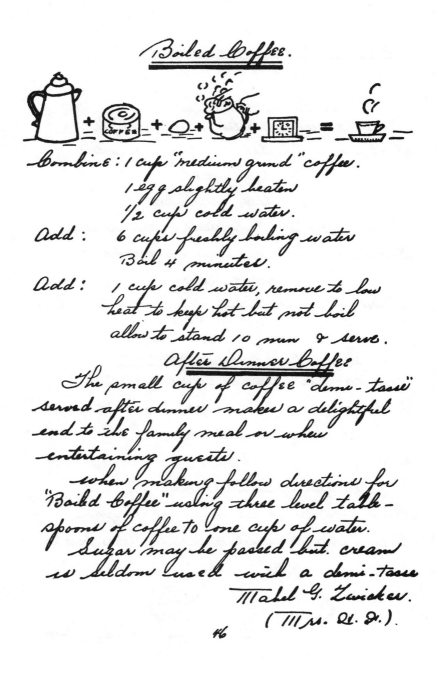

Combine: 1 cup "medium grind" coffee.
1 egg slightly beaten
½ cup cold water.

Add: 6 cups freshly boiling water
Boil 4 minutes.

Add: 1 cup cold water, remove to low
heat to keep hot but not boil
allow to stand 10 min & serve.

After Dinner Coffee

The small cup of coffee "demi-tasse"
served after dinner makes a delightful
end to the family meal or when
entertaining guests.

When making follow directions for
"Boiled Coffee" using three level tablespoons of coffee to one cup of water.

Sugar may be passed but cream
is seldom used with a demi-tasse

Mabel G. Zwicker.

(Mrs. Qt. Dr.).

46

Soups
AND Chowders

Beef Soup Stock

Saw in half: 1 lb. beef shank

Add: 5 oz. lean beef

BROWN IN OVEN.

Add bones to: 2 qt. cold water
BRING to boil. SKIM.

Add: 3/4 tsp. salt
pepper
celery tops
1 onion, sliced

SIMMER GENTLY for four hours.

MAE GLOVER.
(MRS FRED)

Noodle Soup.

3 or 4 lb. fowl, or beef.
1 cup diced carrots.
1 small onion.
½ cup celery.
1 tablespoon salt.
Cover fowl with water & simmer slowly.
When fowl is almost cooked add the
onion, and diced carrots.
Make noodles a couple hours before
required. Method — 2 eggs. ½ teaspoon
salt, and flour enough to make
a stiff dough, then cut in two pieces,
flour each well, and roll on Baking
board as thin as possible, let dry for
two hours, then flour, roll up like
a jelly roll, and cut in thin shreds.
Separate well before putting in broth.
Add chopped celery.
Boil noodles about five or ten minutes.

Beef Tea.

1 lb. lean beefsteak cut in tiny
pieces. add 3 cups of cold water,
simmer on back of stove for two hours.
If desired add some chopped up
celery, and 1 teaspoon salt.

Mary C. Oxner.
(Mrs. S. W.)

— 49 —

Hodge-Podge

2 lbs lamb cut in 2 in cubes
1 lb green beans 1 lb wax beans
4 potatoes quartered
4 carrots
1 quart green peas
¼ teasp pepper 2 teasp salt
9 cups cold water
½ cup browned flour
Wash lamb add water + cook 1 hour
add beans, carrots + potatoes cook
25 min. add peas + cook until
tender Stir flour in heavy
pan until light brown + add
to rapidly boiling vegetables.

— Frances Himmelman
(Mrs. H. B)

Dry Bean Soup

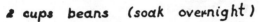

2½ lb. ham bone
4 qts. cold water
1 large onion
1 tsp. pepper
1 tbsp. dried celery leaves
2 cups beans (soak overnight)
2 medium size carrots (diced)
3 large potatoes

Put ham bone, pepper and water in large pot. Add beans and cook slowly 2 hours. Add onion, carrots and celery. Cook slowly 1 hour. Add potatoes. When potatoes are done, soup ready to serve.

Note. Dry or split peas may be used instead of beans

Ada L. Tanner
(Mrs. G. P.)

Corn Chowder.

3 medium potatoes
1 small onion
1 c. water
¼ c. butter
1½ c. canned corn
4 c. milk
Salt and pepper.

Pare and dice potato. Grate onion.
Add water and butter. Simmer until
tender. Add corn and milk, simmer
15 mn. Season with salt and pepper.
If desired, garnish with chopped chives

Alice Adams.
(Mrs. E. C. Adams)

~ Fish Chowder ~

Sauté one-eighth pound fat salt pork - Remove scraps allowing fat to remain in pot Add two large onions finely chopped. Three medium size potatoes cut into small pieces 1½ lbs. haddock fillets or halibut. ½ cup boiling water. Simmer slowly twenty minutes. Add one large can evaporated milk (undiluted) - 1½ cups whole milk - Season to taste, adding pork scraps previously removed. Do not boil after adding milk

Amy Butler ~

Lobster Chowder

2 cups lobsters
1 medium onion
2 medium potatoes
1 pt whole milk
1 small tin evap. milk
butter size of egg
1 tsp. salt; 1/4 tsp. pepper

Cook onion and potato in 1 cup water. When nearly done add lobster cut in pieces. Add salt and pepper, boil 5 minutes. Add milk and butter. Heat to boiling point. Serve piping hot with crisp crackers. Serves 4

Lois J. Hammelman
(Mrs Thomas)

54

Bread and Rolls

White Bread.

4 cups warm water
2 yeast cakes.
2 tbsp. salt.
6 tbsp sugar.
3 tbsp. shortening.
about 11 cups flour.

Method —

Soak yeast cakes in warm water. To which has been added 1 tsp. sugar.

To the warm water add melted shortening. yeast cakes. Sugar and salt. Then add sifted flour and knead until light and elastic.

Put aside in a warm place free from draught until it has doubled in bulk — then knead again. form into loaves. and put in greased pans. (three)

It is important that water be luke warm —

Bake for one hour. in oven pre-heated to 400°. for 15 minutes then reduce to 350° to finish baking.

(Mrs. W. P.) Mildred G. Potter

56

Brown Bread

Scald 2 cups rolled oats, with
1¾ cups of water
When warm add, 1 cup molasses
1 yeast cake in 1 cup of warm water
7½ cups flour, 2 tbsp salt
Mix with, 1¾ cups of warm water, mix
well together, let rise over night,
or do first thing in the morning, let rise
to over double its size, then put in
two good size loaf pans, let rise to
top of pans, bake in oven of 350°
for 1½ hours. Grease top of loaves
with butter when done.

Jean Burns Smith
(Mrs. Malcolm)

Whole Wheat Bread.

1½ cups white flour (sifted)
2 cups whole wheat flour
1 tsp. salt
⅛ cup brown sugar
1½ tbsp. shortening
1 cup hot water
¼ cup warm water
1 yeast cake

Soften yeast in warm water. Put sugar shortening and salt in bowl, and pour hot water over all. Cool. Add yeast and flours. Kneed dough for 10 minutes. Put in greased bowl, and let rise till double in bulk. Punch down and knead well.

Form in loaves, and place in greased pans. Let rise, and bake in moderate oven for 1 hour.

Lillian E. Thurlow
(Mrs S. L.)
58

RAISIN BREAD

1 yeast Cake
1 cup lukewarm water
1 cup milk (scalded and cooled)
1 Tbsp. sugar
1 tsp. salt
6 cups sifted flour
½ cup butter or shortening
1¼ cups sugar
1½ cups Raisins
1 tsp. grated nutmeg
1 tsp. lemon extract
1½ tsp. vanilla

Dissolve yeast and 1 Tbsp. sugar in liquid. Add 2 cups flour — butter and sugar well creamed — and beat until smooth. Let rise in a warm place until light. Add well floured raisins and other ingredients. Knead lightly. Place in well greased bowl and let rise until double in bulk. Mould into loaves and let rise until light. Glaze with egg diluted with water and bake 50 - 60 minutes in 325° oven.

Antoinette E. Smith
(Mrs. B.C.)

59

Steamed Brown Bread

1 cup all-purpose flour
1 cup whole wheat flour
1 cup corn meal
½ cup granulated sugar
1½ teaspoons salt
1 teaspoon baking soda
½ cup molasses
1½ cup sour milk
2 Tablespoons melted shortening

Measure and mix the dry ingredients, add molasses and sour milk. Mix well and add shortening. Pour into greased molds filling ⅔ full.
Cover with waxed paper.
Steam three hours.

Florence L. Eiserlaner
60 (Mrs. C. R.)

Orange Raisin Bread

1 yeast cake dissolved
in ½ cup warm water.
¼ cup unstrained
orange juice
2 tsps grated lemon
rind
1 tbsp. sugar
½ cup raisins
1 egg beaten
1 ¾ cups. sifted flour.

Combine orange juice, rind
and sugar Simmer for five
minutes, over low heat.
Remove from fire and add
raisins. Allow to cool
Add beaten egg and yeast.
Mix well add add flour
mixing for five minutes
Knead, put to rise, shape and
put to rise again.
Bake as for plain   Dorothy Mosher
        bread   (Mrs. P H.)

61

Christmas Stollen

1 cup milk
1 small cup sugar
3/4 cup butter or shortening
2 rounded tsp salt
1 pkg or cake yeast
1/4 cup lukewarm water
2 eggs well beaten
4 1/2 to 5 cups sifted flour
2 tsp. grated lemon rind
1/2 tsp nutmeg
1 cup seeded raisins
1/2 cup mixed candied peel
1/2 cup halved candied cherries

Scald milk, add sugar, shortening and salt. Dissolve yeast in lukewarm water. Cool the milk, add yeast and beaten eggs. Add flour, nutmeg and lemon rind. Knead well. Cover. Let it rise in warm place until double in bulk. Punch down. Work all the fruits into dough. Shape into 2 long oval loaves about 2 in. thick. Place in sheet cake pan with space between loaves. brush with melted butter. Let rise again. Bake in 325° oven for 50 to 60 min. When baked, brush with the following:- 2 tbsp. milk, 2 tsp sugar, a few drops vanilla.

May Eisenhauer (Mrs D.M.)
62

Dark Nut Bread

2 cups. white flour.
2 cups. graham flour.
1/2 cup. molasses.
1 tsp. salt
2 cups. milk
1/2 cup. brown sugar
1/2 cup. chopped nuts
1 tsp. soda dissolved
in molasses.

Raise one hour.
Bake one hour

— A Kinley.

Orange Cranberry Bread

2 cups Flour sifted twice
1 tsp. Salt
1½ tsp. Baking Powder
½ tsp. Soda
1 cup Sugar.

To juice and rind of one orange add 2 tbsp. melted butter and add boiling water to make 3/4 cup liquid. Add to this one beaten egg, and add to dry ingredients. Add one cup chopped walnuts and one cup raw cranberries cut in half

Bake for one hour in 325° oven.

Barbara Mosher
(Mrs. Douglas)

Pineapple and Nut Bread

2¾ cups sifted bread flour
¾ cup brown sugar
½ tsp. salt
3 tsps. baking powder
½ tsp. baking soda
1 cup breakfast bran
¾ cup chopped nuts
1½ cups crushed pineapple (undrained)
1 egg beaten
⅓ cup melted butter or shortening

Method,

Sift together flour, salt b. p. and soda
add nuts and bran, Combine the
beaten egg, with the pineapple, and
add to dry ingredients, add butter lastly.

Bake in moderate oven about 1 hr.

Sadie A. Krickle
(Mrs J. R.)

Date and Nut Bread

1 (1b) package dates
2 tsp. soda
3 tbsp. butter
1 cup sugar
2 eggs
3 cups flour, tsp salt.
1 cup chopped walnuts
1 tsp. vanilla

Method —
Cut dates in halves, cover with boiling water, add soda, set aside to cool.
Cream butter and sugar, add eggs. well beaten, flour. salt and date mixture, walnuts and vanilla.
Bake in a slow oven 1½ hours.

Georgie M. Mason (Mrs. H.F.)

Banana All-Bran Nut Bread

¼ cup shortening
½ cup sugar
1 egg (well-beaten)
1 cup all-bran
1½ cups flour
2 tsps Baking powder

1½ cups mashed bananas
½ tsp. salt
½ tsp. soda
½ cup chopped nut meats
2 tbsps. water
1 tsp. vanilla

Cream shortening and sugar well
Add egg and all-bran, sift flour
with baking powder, salt and soda.
Mix nuts with flour, add with
banana. to which the water has
been added. Stir in vanilla. Pour
in greased loaf tin and let stand
30 minutes. Bake in moderate oven

Hazel Allen
(Mrs. Robert)

67

Refrigerator Rolls

2 cakes compressed yeast
¼ cup sugar
2½ cups lukewarm water
8 cups sifted Robin Hood flour
1 tablespoon salt
2 eggs
2 tablespoons shortening

Method:

Dissolve yeast and sugar in ½ cup lukewarm water. Sift flour, measure, add salt. Add the beaten eggs and dissolved yeast to the remaining 2 cups of water. Gradually add half the flour, then the melted shortening. Gradually beat in the rest of the flour and knead the dough on a lightly floured board until smooth. Place dough in a greased bowl; brush the top with melted butter or other shortening. Cover closely. Keep in Refrigerator until needed, then cut off the amount of dough required and shape into rolls. Let rise in a warm place until light. Bake in moderately hot oven. This dough may be kept in the Refrigerator for 6 or 7 days and small amounts used as required. Knead down occasionally to prevent rising.

Elsie Hemmelman
(Mrs George)

68

CLOVER LEAF ROLLS

    1 pint scalded milk
    2 tbsps. butter
    2 tbsps. sugar
    1½ tsps. salt

Mix and cool to lukewarm.
Add

    1 yeast cake dissolved in
    ¼ cup lukewarm water
    1 white of egg, beaten stiff
    6 cups of flour

Requires about 3 hours to rise. Then put in cupcake tins, 3 little balls in each tin, putting piece of butter in between. Allow to rise until about double in size. Half this quantity makes quite a number. Bake in moderate oven 20 or 25 minutes.

             Jennie C. Knodell

Hot-Cross Buns

2 Yeast Cakes
2 Tbsp Sugar
2 cups Milk
2 Eggs
½ cup Butter
⅔ cup Sugar
7½ cups Sifted Flour
2 tsp. Salt
1½ cups Raisins
¼ tsp Nutmeg

(one a penny)

2 Tbsp. Chopped Candied Cherries (optional)

Dissolve Yeast Cakes and 2 Tbsp Sugar in ½ cup water (warm). Add 2 cups cooled scalded milk. Add ¾ cup flour and beat. Let rise 1 hour. Cream butter and sugar. Beat eggs and add to sponge. Add remaining ingredients and knead lightly. Let rise 2 hours or until double in bulk. Roll dough to ¾ inch thickness and cut with 2½ inch Cookie cutter. Put on greased baking sheet 2 inches apart and let rise 1 hour. Brush rolls with beaten egg white & 1 Tbsp. water. Bake in 325° oven 20 mins. Brush again with egg white and bake 5 mins. longer. When nearly cool top with stiff confectioners Icing in shape of a cross. Serve warm.

Antoinette E. Smith (Mrs. B.E.)

Cinnamon Rolls

1 yeast cake
1/2 cup lukewarm water
1 tsp. sugar
5 cups flour
1 tsp. salt
2 heaping T. crisco
1 tsp. lemon
1/2 cup seedless raisins
3/4 cup sugar

Add yeast and 1 tsp. sugar to lukewarm water. Let stand 5 minutes. Blend all dry ingredients, add yeast mixture and enough lukewarm water to mix to a moderately soft dough. Let rise to double in bulk. Put dough on slightly floured board, cut in two and roll in oblong pieces 1/4 inch thick. Spread with the following mixture creamed to a soft paste.

3 oz butter   1 T. cinnamon
        1 1/2 cups brown sugar

Roll like jelly roll and cut in 1 inch pieces. Stand on ends in buttered pan. Let rise and bake 25 to 30 minutes in 400°F oven. Remove from oven and brush with very thin icing of brown sugar and water boiled to a syrup. Lois J. Himmelman (Mrs Thomas)

91

To Knead Yeast Rising Twists.

Combine.—

    1/2 c. shortening.
    3 tbsps sugar.
    1/2 tsp salt.
    1 tsp vanilla.
    1/2 c. scalded milk.

Add.— 2 yeast cakes, dissolved in
    1/2 c. warm water.

Blend in.— 1 1/2 c. flour, and beat until
    smooth. Cover and let rise
    for 15 minutes.

Add.— 3 eggs, one at a time, beating
    well after each addition.

Blend in — 1 1/2 c. flour, & mix thoroughly

Let rise.— Let covered dough in a
    warm place (80 to 90 °F)
    about 1 1/2 hour
    (Dough will be quite soft.)

Combine — 3/4 c. chopped nuts }
    1/2 c. sugar.   } nut mixture
    1 tsp. cinnamon.   }

Divide — dough in small pieces (1 tbsp)
    Roll in nut mixture. Stretch
    To about 8 inch lengths. Twist
    in desired shapes. Place on
    greased baking sheet.
        Let stand five minutes.

Bake.— In moderate oven (375.° F)
    for 12 – 15 minutes.

Serve hot.   Mabel G. Zwicker.
    72 (Mrs. N. H.)

Butterscotch Pinwheels

3 c. flour
6 tsp. B. P.
6 " butter or more
1 tsp. salt.
milk to roll out.

Sift flour. B. P. and salt
cut in butter, add milk to
form a dough to roll out
Roll fairly thin, spread with
1 c. t. sugar and 3 tbsp
butter mixed together and
roll like a jelly roll.
slice and bake in hot oven.

Mary G. Duff.

Tea Ring

Cream 3 tbsp. (heaping) shortening
  1/4 c. sugar.
Add 1 egg beaten; 1 yeast cake
dissolved in 1/2 c. luke warm water
1/2 c scalded milk (cooled)
3 1/2 c. sifted flour & salt.
Mix & let stand in a warm place
for 2 hrs. or more to raise.
Roll out 1/4 inch thickness
brush well with melted
butter or shortening, cover
with cinnamon, brown
sugar & raisins.
Roll up like a jelly roll, put ends
together to form a ring.
Let rise 30 minutes or more, then
bake 30 minutes in moderate oven.
Ice when cool.
It is much easier to handle if you
cut your dough in half and
make two rings.

Kate L. Corkum.
(Mrs. W. A.)

74

Tea Biscuits

2½ cups white flour
3 tsp. baking powder
½ cup butter or shortening
½ tsp. salt
¾ cup cold milk or milk and water

Sift flour, baking powder and salt. Add butter and shortening. Then add milk or water. Mix and put dough on floured board. Roll lightly. Cut with biscuit cutter. Bake on a buttered sheet in hot oven (400°) about fifteen minutes.

Hot Cake

Use rich biscuit dough baked in cake pan. When taken from oven cut in two layers, spread generously with butter and sprinkle with brown sugar and nutmeg. Replace top layer, then cut in squares and serve.

Lilla Knickle

Twin Mountain Muffins

1/3 cup butter 1/4 cup sugar
1 egg 3/4 cups milk, 2 cups flour
3 tsp B Powder
Cream butter, sugar, add unbeaten
egg beat well slowly add milk
lastly flour with B Powder
fill muffin tins 3/4 full bake 1/2 hour.

Stella A. Holmes
(Mrs J A)

The Misses Duff's Braco Scones

1 cup flour 1 dessert-spoon
B Powder pinch salt.
Combine and sieve into bowl
add milk until consistency of
B Powder biscuits divide into
round cakes and cook on griddle.

Date Muffins

Chop coarsely one cupful of dates. Sift together two cups of flour, one-half teaspoon of salt and two teaspoons of baking powder. Rub one large tablespoon of butter into the flour. Add the dates, one well beaten egg, one and one-third cups of milk, and mix to a stiff batter. Bake in hot, well greased muffin pans in a moderate oven for about twenty minutes.

These muffins may be topped with whipped cream for a dessert.

Marion Adams

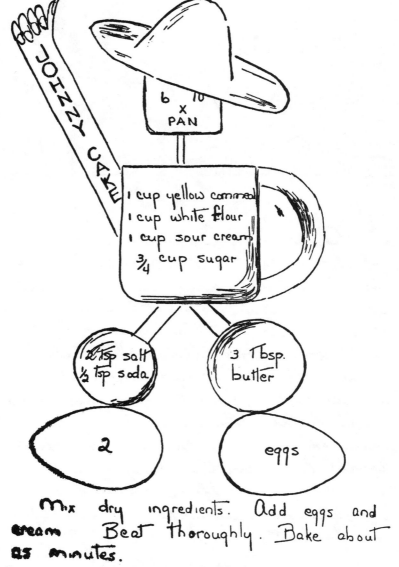

JOHNNY CAKE

6 × 10
X
PAN

1 cup yellow cornmeal
1 cup white flour
1 cup sour cream
3/4 cup sugar

2 tsp salt
1/2 tsp soda

3 Tbsp.
butter

2

eggs

Mix dry ingredients. Add eggs and cream. Beat thoroughly. Bake about 25 minutes.

May Eisenhauer (Mrs. D.M.)

98

Fish

Important Principles of Fish Cookery.

1. Serve adequate portions of fish as a main course. 1 lb. of boneless fish (salt, smoked or fresh) is a minimum for 3 persons. It is a delicious, economical, easily digested, complete protein food, not a flavouring, nor a penance to eat. Not all the meats and fowl can excel fisheries products in nutritive variety for any day or meal.

2. Season before rather than after cooking. Lemon juice plus salt is far better used to marinate fresh fish for upwards of 2 hrs. before cooking than as the inevitable lemon point foisted upon us at table. It both flavours and seals the juices. With smoked fish substitute half milk and water. Almost every herb, spice or seasoning has been, and can be, used with advantage at this time, either singly or in combination, as the type of fish or inspiration may dictate. The important point is that strong or inappropriate sauces and seasoning are relics of bygone days when quality was questionable at times. Don't disguise fish, shellfish or crustacea. Allow the many appealing nuances of flavour to stand on their own with just that degree of pointing up or delicate blending which the other flavours and bouquets in marinade or sauce provide. Herein lies the art of seasoning. Be creative, not a slave to a recipe. After poaching or steaming try a real Hollandaise Sauce, plain or slightly seasoned, or better still a Mousseline Sauce (1 part whipped cream, 2 parts Hollandaise). This latter may be used for hot or cold fish. Leave the glutinous white sauces for the prosaic souls. For a grilled, baked or fried fish what can be nicer than a plain butter sauce with a garnish, and perhaps a bit of mushroom, or a contribution of lobster purée or oyster liquor? Must our gastronomic horizon be ever riddened with the lowly tomato in

80

(cont. next page)

manifold variety?

3. Do not <u>overcook</u>. Fish has no coarse fibre requiring softening. The delicate flesh must only be "set" (like a poached or coddled egg) at which time the muscle flakes start to separate, and the bones if any begin to loosen. Test with a fork. Overcooking produces a consistency resembling moist blotting paper.

4. <u>Methods and times</u>. (a) <u>Boiling</u> is a misnomer. Fish should be gently simmered only. Wrapping in parchment or cheesecloth is a makeshift. Get a fish boiler if you may, and limit the method to fatty fish. (b) <u>Poaching</u> (as you would an egg) means simmering gently in a covered pan with less fluid, containing lemon juice and seasoning. With smoked fish use seasoned milk and water. (c) <u>Steaming</u> (<u>never</u> in a pressure cooker) preserves flavour better than boiling and fish breaks less. An excellent method for delicately flavoured fish. (d) <u>Baking</u>. Temperature should be 450°. Lower temperatures cause the juices to run and fish to dry out. Baste very frequently with fat. Use no water. (e) <u>To Grill</u> first preheat oven to 450°. Have plenty of fat over the fish. (f) <u>Frying</u> may be in deep fat at 375°, usually in a batter, or pan frying in smaller or greater quantities of fat, usually after dipping first in milk or egg then in crumbs or cornmeal. (g) For <u>chowders</u>, bisques, soups, curries or à la newburghs add fish pieces to seasoned base last and poach only. If using cooked pieces heat through only. Stir <u>very gently</u>. <u>Average times</u> <u>for cooking</u> are easy to remember: <u>10 min per inch</u> <u>of thickness</u> for any above method, with the following exceptions, 2 min more for fatty fleshed fish, 5 min. more if fish is wrapped in parchment or foil, and 10 min. more if hard frozen (less if only partly frozen. Steaming time, generally longer,

81

(cont next page)

is variable according to procedure. To accomplish uniformity of cooking throughout by any method it is advisable to trim thin ends and sides of fillets, reserving these for chowders & casserole dishes

5. Salt Fish is a ~~great~~ ~~delicacy~~ requiring special treatment. It is little-known to so many people because disliking excess salt they do not understand that it may be easily removed by adequate soaking, leaving a flesh of very delightful texture and flavour. Being salted for preservation immediately after catching, no fish can have more of that fresh-caught taste. Whole fish, or boneless, should be so divided that the thick portions are reserved for poaching or grilling and thin bits used for made-up dishes. Skin the whole fish befor. breaking up. With the fingers open up the surface slightly on the thick portions. Soak in plenty of water ~~two~~ to four hours. Drain. Replace water with half milk and half water and 1 tsp. of sugar. Soak overnight (10 hours) or longer. Change if desired (milk extracts salt better than water). Parboiling toughens the flesh. Then with the thick pieces proceed as suggested in para. 2 above, and bake, poach or broil. 'Tis truly a feast for the gods! The thin bits may be drained dry, dusted in a bag with flour, and fried gently with pork scraps or bacon, and so served. Or for that zestful simple item "quickie" meal or unsurpassed party fare, combine lightly poached bits with equal parts of hot mashed potatoes, bind with egg, season gently with mace, garlic, chives (or onion), parsley, finely grated lemon peel, basil, salt, pepper & melted butter. Whip thoroughly & when cold fashion in 1 inch spheres & coat with crumbs or cornmeal. French fry when required. Serve hot out of hand with drinks hot or cold — nothing more. (who would crave another thing, so you had better prepare plenty.)

                                    — Arthur James —

General Hints for Frying Fish

Wash fish and dry it thoroughly

Dip fish in beaten egg and roll in fine cracker crumbs.

Melt mixture of butter and shortening in hot frying pan and place fish in it. Sprinkle with salt and pepper and fry until brown.

This method is particularly good for haddock fillets, halibut, filet of sole, scallops and clams.

Mackerel, smelt or trout may be rolled in seasoned flour or cornmeal and fried!

Gertrude Stoddard
(Mrs. C.J.)

83

Haddock with Mushroom Sauce

2 lbs. Haddock
1 can mushroom soup
¼ cup light cream
½ cup grated cheese
½ teaspoon grated onion
  Dash of pepper & paprika

Place haddock in greased baking dish.
Combine soup, cream, cheese, onion
and pepper. Pour over fish and
sprinkle with paprika. Bake in hot
oven (400°F) 25 to 30 minutes. Serve
with lettuce and tomato salad.
Makes 4 or 5 servings.

Baked Halibut or Haddock

2 lbs. Halibut
1 cup milk
1 large onion
3 or 4 thin slices of salt pork
1 tablespoon flour
1 tablespoon butter

Place halibut or haddock in greased
baking dish. Place strips of pork on fish,
also sliced onion, pepper, salt and
milk. Sprinkle flour all over fish.
Bake in hot oven, basting occasionally
while baking.
        Elsie Himmelman
      Mrs George)
        84

Baked Stuffed Haddock or Halibut

Clean about one 4 lb. haddock
or halibut. Sprinkle with salt,
then stuff with

$\frac{1}{2}$ cup cracker crumbs

$\frac{3}{4}$ cup melted butter

few drops onion juice

$\frac{1}{2}$ cup stale bread crumbs

$\frac{3}{4}$ tsp salt and pepper

$\frac{3}{4}$ cup hot water

Put strips of bacon on fish, add
a little water to the pan, bake
in hot oven one hour. If desired
serve with white sauce and garnish
with lemon.

Mona G. Rhodenizer
(Mrs H. H.)

85

= Soused Mackerel =
Clean, split open
and cut the fresh mack-
erel into servings.
Arrange in layers in
baking dish with a
few whole spices and
shake of pepper and salt.
Just cover with vinegar
and dot top with 1 tbsp butter.
Bake about 30 mins. Good hot
or cold.
Fresh herring may be baked likewise.

= Boiled Mackerel with Sauce =

Sprinkle salt on fresh mackerel and let stand over night.

Put on to simmer in cold
water with little onion.

Make white sauce with 1c.
fish broth, 1c rich milk, 1 tbsp
butter, 2 tbsp flour & pepper.

Remove fish to platter. Cover
with sauce and vinegar to
taste.

Lillian Moher
(Mrs Stephen)

86

the one and only
Bluenose

Queen of the North Atlantic, - and
International Champion Fishing Schooner
Built in, and sailed out of Lunenburg
by her famous Capt. Angus Walters

Boiled Salt Herring and Potatoes

Soak herring over night. Next day clean herring. Wash and ring potatoes, boil, and about 15 minutes before potatoes are done lay herring on top of potatoes and cook until done.

Soused Herring or Mackerel

Clean fresh herring or mackerel, place in shallow baking dish. Make a mixture of vinegar, enough to cover fish, and add sugar, pepper, and salt to taste and about a tablespoon of mixed pickling spice. Bake in oven until tender. Serve when cold with boiled or baked potatoes.

Katherine B. Bourque
(Mrs. D. J.)

88

Creamed Finnan Haddie

Cover a finnan haddie with water, let come to the boiling point and simmer for a few minutes until the fish is cooked - using the top of the stove or oven. Drain the fish, lay on a hot platter and place small pieces of butter on top. Return to the oven to heat and just before serving add ½ cup of cream or milk heated. Do not leave too long in oven or the cream or milk may curdle from the smoked fish. Garnish with parsley if desired.

Baked Finnan Haddie.

Skin a 2½ lbs. finnan haddie. cut in pieces serving size. Place in baking dish face up. place small pieces of butter on top. partly cover with milk and cream. pepper and onions if desired.
- Bake half hour in moderate oven.

Mabel Crouse
(Mrs. Moyle)

Fried Fish Cheeks

1 lb. fresh fish cheeks
1 egg (beaten)
1 cup rolled Corn
Flakes
                Salt & pepper

Wash fish cheeks and dry
thoroughly. Dip in beaten
egg, seasoned with salt & pepper.
Roll in crushed Corn Flakes,
place cheeks in hot greased
frying pan. Brown on both
sides. Cooking time ten to
fifteen minutes.

                Kay Ritcey
                (Mrs L. J.)
90

KIPPERED / HERRING

Pour boiling water over herring
Let stand five minutes. Drain.
Place a bit of butter on each one..
Place in a very hot oven until
edges curl — about three minutes.
Serve with toast or baked
potatoes.

91 Evelyn U. B. Rice
(Mrs. C. B.)

Broiled Smelt

¼ cup butter, melted   ¼ tsp pepper
1 tbsp. lemon juice   1 pound smelt
1 tsp. salt   ½ cup flour

Mix butter, lemon juice, salt and pepper.
Clean smelt. Dip each in butter mixture,
Then roll in flour
Place in double broiler rack, and
broil in minutes, turning once.

Fried Eels.

Cut eels in any desired lengths
Place in pan and cover with water.
Add salt. Let come to a boil, pour
off water and clean.
Place on board To dry.
Dip in melted butter, then flour,
and fry brown.   Gertrude Whynacht
(Mrs. W. A.)

92

Baked Fish Fillets

1½ lb. fish fillets
6 tbsp. butter
3 tbsp. chopped onion
¾ cup tomato ketchup
¾ cup hot water
½ tsp. pepper
1⅓ tsp. salt
grated cheese - chopped parsley

Place fish in shallow baking pan. Sprinkle cheese over fish. Mix butter, onion, salt, pepper, parsley, tomato ketchup and hot water. Pour over fish and bake in moderate oven.

Florence E. Hewat
(Mrs. W. A.)

Baked Fillets

Roll 1 or 2 lbs. fresh cod or haddock fillets in flour, and place on baking pan. To 3 beaten eggs add $\frac{1}{2}$ c. milk or cream, small piece of butter, salt and pepper to taste. Pour mixture over fish. Bake $\frac{1}{2}$ hr. in hot oven, dot with butter and serve with lemon slices.

Jean Whynacht
94 (Mrs. R. M.)

Baked Scallops on Half Shell.

Clean the scallops and arrange one or more on each half shell. To each one add one teaspoon bread crumbs, one tablespoon cream, a dot of butter and dash of salt and pepper. Bake in 375° oven 30 minutes or until brown. Potatoes diced and arranged around scallops on shell if desired and baked at the same time. Clams may be baked in the same manner, arranging two or three clams on each half shell.

Baked scallops or Lobster in casserole.

Grease baking dish and cover with thin layer of bread crumbs. Place 1 lb. scallops or meat from 1 good sized lobster broken into edible sized pieces. Season with salt & pepper and add milk to level of top of fish (Do not cover). Dot top generously with butter. Melt butter size of an egg and add the crumbs from a thick slice of bread. Arrange buttered crumbs on top of fish and place in 350° oven. Bake scallops about ¾ hour and lobsters until crumbs are brown. Serves 3.

Jennie M. Smeltzer.
(Mrs. E. S.)

95

Tender Brown Scallops

1/2 tsp. salt

few grains pepper

few grains cayenne

1 s̶i̶f̶t̶e̶d̶ crumbs

1 egg

2 tbsps. water

1 1/2 lbs. scallops

4 tbsps melted
butter

Mix salt, pepper, cayenne and crumbs together. Then beat egg and water with a fork and dip each scallop first in crumbs, then egg mixture and again in crumbs. Put in medium baking dish and let stand for about 30 min. for coating to set or harden. Start your oven at 450°. Pour melted butter over scallops and bake 25 to 30 min. or until scallops are richly brown and crisp on the outside. Serve with Tartar Sauce (below)

1 med. dill pickle

1 tbsp. capers

3 sprigs parsley

1 c. mayonnaise (scant)

1 1/2 tbsps prepared mustard

1/2 small onion

Chop up pickle and capers as fine as possible. Cut parsley and onion and mix into mayonnaise with all ingredients.

(Mrs. G. Ray) Jean D. Lohnes

Escalloped Lobster

Split cooked lobsters in two and remove the entrails. Dice meat, being careful to remove all the meat from the claws. Prepare gravy by mixing equal parts of milk and cream, thickened with 2 heaping tablespoonful of flour, creamed with 2 tablespoonful of butter. Season well with salt, pepper and a tiny pinch of grated nutmeg. Add lobster to sauce and place in buttered dish. Cover with bread crumbs and place in hot oven for 10 minutes to brown.

Jean B. Burke
(Mrs. Archie)

Lobster a la Newberg.

2 cups prepared lobster.
4 tbsp. butter.
4 tbsp. sherry.
4 egg yolks.
1 cup cream
1 tsp. salt.

½ tsp. paprika and a pinch of nutmeg and pepper.

Melt butter in top of double boiler. add paprika and lobster meat. heat thoroughly, covered, stirring occasionally with a fork —

Gently stir in sherry.

Beat egg yolks. and stir in cream

Just before serving time. stir the egg yolk and cream mixture with the lobster. add salt and pepper, then stir constantly over hot water until creamy —

Serve immediately. Serves 6.

(Mrs. W. P.) Mildred P. Potter.

Lobster Rarebit

Shell and chop about 2c.
freshly boiled lobster meat.

Make a sauce in double-boiler
of following :-

3 tbsp butter $\frac{1}{4}$ tsp chopped onion

1 tbsp flour $\frac{1}{2}$ tsp salt

$\frac{1}{2}$ tsp mustard $\frac{1}{8}$ tsp pepper

1 c. cream

Add lobster to hot sauce.
Cover with grated cheese, brown in
oven. Serve with toast.

Ethel F. Mosher.
(Mrs Daniel)

Room
Board

99

Codfish Souffle

1 cup cold cooked salt codfish picked
fine. Mix with:
1 cup mashed potatoes and season with
salt and pepper. Add:
1 beaten egg
⅓ cup milk
1 tbsp. butter
Put in buttered dish, let stand in
oven till very hot. Beat white and
yolk of another egg separately. Beat
white very stiff, add salt & pepper
to yolk, combine white and yolk,
heap over fish and brown in oven.

Codfish & Cheese

Freshen a pound of salt codfish,
then let it come to a boil. Pick
in flakes; season with pepper. Prepare
a white sauce; mix with picked fish,
add one beaten egg. Pour in greased
baking dish, spread grated cheese
thickly on top. Bake in oven
until a delicate brown.

Bessie S. Iversen
(Mrs. L.J.)

Creamed Salt Codfish.

½ c. salt codfish
1 c. rich milk
1 tbsp. flour
1 tbsp. butter

1 egg
1 tsp. parsley
pepper

Shred and soak fish over night. Simmer gently for 15 min. Add milk. Rub flour smooth in butter, and add to hot mixture with the minced egg (which had been hard boiled) then add pepper and minced parsley.

Can be served on toast or as a luncheon dish.

Mildred K. Rundle
(Mrs A. C.)

101

Shredded Codfish

1 pkg. codfish
2 c. mashed potatoes
1 pint cream or milk
2 eggs (beaten)
½ c. butter
Season to taste.
Mix together in batter.
Bake for 25 or 30 minutes.

J. E. Duff.
(Mrs. William)

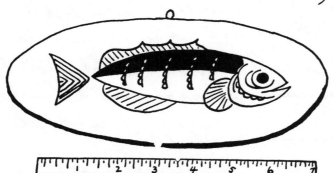

Salmon Loaf

1 large can salmon

$\frac{1}{3}$ cup milk

$\frac{2}{3}$ cup soft bread crumbs

1 tbsp. parsley

1 tsp. salt

1 tbsp. lemon juice

2 eggs

Cook bread crumbs in double boiler for five minutes. Stir in unbeaten eggs, seasoning and fish. Turn into greased pan and bake in 350 degree oven for forty-five to sixty minutes.

Ada L. Tanner

(Mrs. G. P.)

Fish Soufflé

3½ tbsp. Butter
3½ tbsp. Flour
2 cups Milk
⅛ tsp. Paprika
⅔ tsp. Salt
⅓ cup Bread Crumbs.
2 cups Cooked Fish
2 Eggs.

Melt butter, add flour and when smooth
stir in milk. Cook until thickened
add seasoning and crumbs. Cool.
Add flaked fish to sauce and mix
well. Stir in egg yolks, and
stiffly beaten whites.
Put in greased baking dish and
bake in moderately hot oven until
firm.

K. Heckman.

FISH SCALLOR

1 Small onion

1 Cup Celery

1 Cup Crabmeat

1 Cup Shrimp

1 Cup Lobster

1 Cup Tuna

1½ Cups Mayonnaise

½ tsp. Salt

- Pepper

- Worcestershire sauce

1 Cup buttered Crumbs

Bake in oven 350° for 20 minutes

Audrey M. Smith
(Mrs. W. W.)
105

Sauce for Fish

Add
- ½ cup chili sauce
- ¼ cup sliced stuffed olives
- ¼ tsp Lea & Perrins sauce

to one cup of mayonnaise

Tartar Sauce

- ¾ cup mayonnaise
- ¼ tbsp. chopped onion
- ½ tbsp. capers
- 1 tbsp. pickles finely chopped
- 1 tbsp. olives "
- 1 tbsp. parsley "
- 1 tbsp. tarragon vinegar

Combine ingredients.

Hollendaise Sauce

- ½ cup butter
- 2 egg yolks
- 1 tbsp lemon juice
- ⅓ cup boiling water
- ¼ tsp. salt
- Dash cayenne

Divide butter in 3 pieces. Put 1 piece in top of double boiler with egg yolks and lemon juice. Cook, stirring constantly until butter is melted. Add second piece of butter and, as mixture thickens, third piece. Add water, cook 1 minute, and season. If mixture curdles, add 2 tbsp. of heavy cream, drop by drop. Just before serving sauce, 2 tbsp. sherry may be added in the same manner, beating constantly.

Hazel Hopgood (Mrs. R St.C)

106

Drawn Butter

⅓ cup butter   2 tbsp flour
1½ cups hot water (or fish stock)
½ tsp salt, little pepper
1 tsp lemon juice

Melt half the butter, add flour with seasoning, and pour on hot water gradually, boil 5 minutes add remaining butter in small pieces before serving

Onion Sauce

2 Medium onions cut fine boil in 1½ cups of water for 10 minutes pinch of salt, piece of butter, thicken with 2 tsp flour mixed in cold water let boil for 5 more minutes

Jean Burns Smith
(Mrs Malcolm)

FISH - FARCE

for Fish Pudding or Cakes or Balls

1 ¾ lbs. Fish (Haddock or Pike)
1 pint cream
1 pint milk
3 ½ ounces Butter
1 Tbsp. Salt
1 ounce Potato Flour
½ tsp. Grated Nutmeg (for those
who like it).

The fish is scraped from the tail towards the head, also the bone. Place on board and scrape lightly to avoid cutting large pieces of fish meat at once. When all is scraped, melt the butter in a saucepan and then put the saucepan in cold water.

The fish meat with the salt is ground once, the potato flour is now added, and the meat is thereupon ground 4 times. The butter (ice cold) is now added teaspoon-wise, while grinding 5 times more, and at the same time add the milk, little by little. The Farce is now put in a bowl, and is battered; while, little by little, adding the cream, which like the milk should have been boiled up the day before. (Remember to add slowly).

The Farce can be looser for pudding than for Balls. For pudding the Farce is filled into a greased mold.

For Sauce, use a mixture of melted butter, flour, cream & fish bouillon, to which boiled shrimps may be added.

Maimy Blom
Glassverkveien 23
Høvik. Baerum, Norway

108

Meat and Fowl

Roast Beef
with Yorkshire Pudding + Horse Radish Sauce.

Roasting Table	Internal Temperature	Time per lb.
Rare	140°F	18-20 min.
Medium	160°F	22-25 min.
Well Done	170°F.	27-35 min.

Dust pan with flour and rub meat with salt. Beef, to be wellroasted should be started in hot oven so that surface may be quickly seared. After flour in pan is browned, reduce heat.

Yorkshire Pudding

3 eggs   1 pt. milk
2/3 cup flour   1 tsp. salt

Method: Beat eggs lightly, add milk; then add mixture gradually to the flour, stirring constantly.

Pour some drippings from the roast beef into another baking pan. Turn dough into it and bake 45 min. Cut in squares and serve around platter.

Horse Radish Sauce

1/4 tsp. salt
1/2 cup Cream (whipped)

Fold horse radish and salt into the whipped cream. (This sauce is very nice served with Baked Ham

BELLE BACKMAN MACK
(Mrs. S.E. Mack.)

110

Roast Pork & Apple Sauce

Wipe pork. Sprinkle with salt
& pepper. Place on rack in roaster
dredge meat & bottom of pan
with flour. Put in moderate oven
375°. Bake 3 or 4 hours, basting
frequently with fat in pan
The usual time is twenty-five
minutes per pound.
Add sliced onion if desired
during the last hour of baking
To make gravy, add small amount
water, & thicken with flour or
corn starch.

Apple Sauce.

Peel, & slice six medium apples
Add 1/2 cup sugar
Cover saucepan, steam over low
heat until creamy, stir frequently
If not tart enough, add a small
amount of lemon Juice.

B. Hazel Smith,
(Mrs. R. M.)

///

Roast Lamb

In selecting lamb be sure that meat is pinkish in color. Lean meat is firm and fine grained and fat is white, hard and flaky.

Select a leg of lamb weighing from 5 to 7 lbs., preferably cut to include some of loin. Wipe with damp cloth, sprinkle with salt and pepper, and rub well with flour. Place on rack in open pan skin side down and cut side up. Roast in oven 450°F. for 30 minutes, reduce heat to 300°F. and bake 2 to 2½ hours. The lower roasting temperature decreases the shrinkage and produces a roast that is less dry.

Mint Jelly

1½ cups water
2 cups mint leaves
1 cup vinegar

1 cup liquid pectin
Green coloring
6½ cups sugar

Mix water, vinegar, mint leaves and enough green coloring to give shade desired, and stir until dissolved. Add sugar and bring to boiling point. Add pectin, boil 1 minute and remove from fire. Let stand 1 minute, skim, remove mint leaves and fill glasses.

Mint Sauce

1 cup finely chopped mint leaves   1 tbsp. powdered sugar
½ cup mild vinegar

Dissolve sugar in vinegar. Pour over mint and let steep 1 hour

Joyce L. Tupper (Mrs. J. A.)

112

Roast Veal

Place leg of veal on rack in open pan, fat side up. Cook uncovered, in a slow oven 325° f. 45 minutes per lb. Do not sear the meat or add water.

Dressing for Meat or Fowl

2 c. fine bread crumbs
2 c. mashed potatoes
1 apple unpeeled (diced)
½ medium sized onion (cut finely)
Butter or margarine, size of an egg
Salt, pepper, sugar to taste.
Herbs, as desired.

Method —

: Brown onion in butter. Mix well, all other ingredients in order given. Mash thoroughly and it is ready for use.

Myrtle Beringer
(Mrs. Benson)

113

Baked Ham

Remove wrapper and let ham stand
at room temperature for ½ hr.
Place on a rack, fat side up, in an
uncovered, shallow baking pan
Do not cover or add water.
Bake in a 325 degree oven.
Whole ham 15 to 18 min. per. lb.
When ham is baked remove from oven
and cut off skin carefully.
Score fat in diamonds with sharp knife.
Cover ham with following glaze.

Ham Glaze

½ cup corn syrup heated and brushed
over ham.
Mixture of 1 cup brown sugar,
1 teaspoon dry mustard and vinegar to
moisten Spread over ham. Stick with cloves

Helen Lynch
(Mrs. W. L.)

114

Raisin Sauce

1 cup of sugar   ½ cup of water or drippings

1 cup raisins, cut in pieces

2 tbsp. butter   3 tbsp. vinegar

1 tbsp. Worcestershire sauce

Few drops Tabasco   1 tsp. salt

¼ tsp. cloves   dash of pepper

Few grains of mace   1 glass fruit jelly

Cook sugar & water 5 min

Add other ingredients & cook until
jelly dissolves.

Helen Lynch
(Mrs. W. L.)

115

Boiled Tongue
with Blackberry Sauce

1 fresh Beef Tongue
Whole Cloves
1 glass Blackberry Jam
1 cup Raisins
Juice of 1 Lemon

Boil tongue until tender, adding 1 bay leaf and ½ cup diced celery to the water while cooking. When tender, remove skin. Trim off root-end and stick the solid meat full of cloves.

Place in a greased baking pan, dust with flour, pour over it the jelly beaten soft with a fork; add raisins which have been cooked until tender in 1 cup of water.

Add lemon juice and bake in a hot oven for 30 minutes, basting often. Serve hot or cold.

(The choicest part of the tongue lies from the root to the middle and should be cut down in thin slices.)

BELLE BACKMAN MACK
(Mr. S. E. Mack.)

116

Pot Pie

Select a 2 lb. piece of beef. Wipe, cut in 2 inch pieces. Place in pot, add cold WATER enough to cover it well. Let cook about ½ hour. Add a large chopped onion, two sliced carrots, six medium potatoes cut in inch pieces.
Add salt to taste, 1 tsp. summer savory.
Simmer 1 hour. Make a dough using 1½ cups flour, 3 tsp. B.P.
Mix with milk or water.
Have dough soft enough to roll on floured board ¼ in. thick.
Cut in small squares and add to soup about 12 minutes before serving as that will be the required time for cooking dough.

B. Hazel Smith.
(Mrs. R.M)

Corn Beef & Cabbage

2 lbs Corn Beef
1 lb lean pork
Cover meat with cold water
simmer for 2½ to 3 hrs.
1 medium head of cabbage, cut in
quarters, put in with meat
the last 20 minutes

To Corn Beef.

1 gal water
1½ lbs fine salt
½ lb brown sugar
½ oz salt petre
Boil for 15 minutes and skim
when cold pour over the beef.
Place heavy weight on meat
to keep under water.
Store in cold basement

Jean Burns Smith
(Mrs. Malcolm)

118

Swiss Steak

2½ lbs. steak.
2 tbsps. fat.
¾ tsp. salt.
Dash of pepper
½ onion
½ cup. flour.
1½ cups. water
½ cup. ketchup

Add salt and pepper to flour and pound into steak. Brown in pan with fat, then add onion, water and ketchup. Cover closely and simmer slowly about 1½ hours. Vegetables may be added if desired.

Dorothy Mosher
(Mrs. P. H.)

119

Steak and Kidney Pie   6 Servings

1 1/2 lbs chuck or round beef.
2 3/ Veal or Lamb Kidneys
3/4 tbsp butter or beef fat
1/3 cups chopped onion
3 cups boiling stock
1/2 Bay leaf.
Flour (for gravy)
Salt and Pepper.
Worcestershire Sauce.
Pie Crust

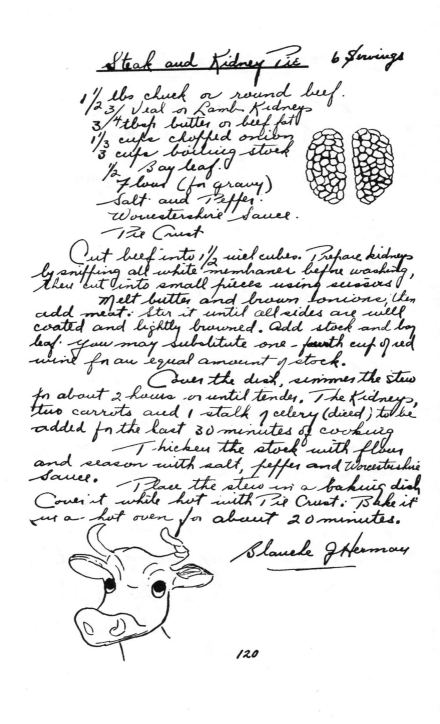

Cut beef into 1 1/2 inch cubes. Prepare kidneys by snipping all white membranes before washing, then cut into small pieces using scissors.

Melt butter and brown onions, then add meat. Stir it until all sides are well coated and lightly browned. Add stock and bay leaf. You may substitute one-fourth cup of red wine for an equal amount of stock.

Cover the dish, simmer the stew for about 2 hours or until tender. The kidneys, two carrots and 1 stalk of celery (diced) to be added for the last 30 minutes of cooking.

Thicken the stock with flour and season with salt, pepper and Worcestershire Sauce. Place the stew in a baking dish. Cover it while hot with Pie Crust. Bake it in a hot oven for about 20 minutes.

Blanche J Herman

120

Braised Liver with Vegetables

1½ lbs beef or calf liver
~~Seasoned~~ flour.
½ cup hot bacon drippings.
2 diced carrots.
2 seeded chopped green peppers.
6 small ~~onions~~.
1 cup sliced celery.
1 cup boiling water or stock.

Cut liver into 1 inch slices. Dredge it with seasoned flour and brown liver in bacon drippings Cover liver with vegetables and add water or stock. Cover it. Simmer the stew for about ¾ hour or until the liver is tender. Add, if necessary more boiling water and seasoning (A calf liver will be tender in about 20 minutes)   6 Servings

Blanche J Herman

HEALTH FOOD GIRLS!!
12!

Barbecued Spareribs.

3 lbs. Spareribs
3 cps. water.
1 cp. vinegar
3/4 cp. minced onion
1 clove
pelled garlic

1 1/2 T. Worchester sauce
1/4 cp. Sugar
3 T. catcup
2 T. salt.
1/4 tsp. pepper
1 Bay leaf.

Broil spareribs which have been chopped into serving size pieces, in oven-broiler until golden brown on each side. Meanwhile combine remaining ingredients and boil for 10 mins. in an uncovered saucepan. Thicken this mixture as you would a gravy. Place spare ribs in an uncovered baking pan or roaster and pour sauce over them. Bake in a hot oven 450° for one hour, basting every 10 mins. Serves 4 or 5.

Elizabeth Winters
(Mrs. C.A.)

122

Sweetbreads

Soak sweetbreads in cold water for 1 hr. Put in stewpan & boil until tender. Let stand until cold. Slice sweetbreads in half, dip in egg & breadcrumbs & fry in hot fat until nicely browned.

Creamed Sweetbreads

Prepare as in previous recipe. Boil with half a dozen mushrooms until tender. Melt 1 tablesp. of butter in top of double boiler & add 1 tablesp. of flour. Mix until smooth. Add ½ pint of cream & stir until thick. Add sweetbreads & mushrooms. Season with salt & a dash of cayenne. Serve on toast or in patty shells.

G. Van de Seul (Whs D.C.)

123

Porcupine Meal Balls.

1 1/2 lbs. hamburg steak
1/2 cup uncooked rice
1 tsp salt.
Pepper
1 tbsp grated onion
1 can tomato soup.
1/2 cup water.

Method; Combine meat, rice, onion, and seasoning and shape into small balls. Heat tomato soup and water, drop in meal balls and cook fifteen minutes in pressure cooker after pressure is up to fifteen pounds.

Hilda M. Young
(Mrs. D. E.)

124

Ham steak with apples.

one thick slice pre. cooked ham.
15 whole cloves
3/4 cup brown sugar
3/4 cup port wine.
4 apples, cored and sliced

Method —

Stud the ham fat with cloves.
Put ham in open roasting pan.
and bake for 25 to 35 minutes in 350° oven

Remove from oven. and spread
ham with sugar — then pour wine
over ham slowly.

Return ham to oven which is
set at 400° — allow 20 minutes for
glazing — now remove ham to hot
platter, and cook apple slices in
syrup left in roasting pan. about
five minutes. turning once. serves 6.

Mrs. W.P. Mildred P. Potter.

125

HAWAIIAN HAM

1 Tbsp. Mustard
1 Tbsp Flour
4 Tbsp. Brown Sugar
1 cup Pineapple Juice
¼ cup weak vinegar
1 slice 1½ inch thick
    Cured Ham.

Cover Ham
with sauce made of
other ingredients and
bake in moderate oven 1 hour,
basting frequently.
10 minutes before finished cooking —
cover with slices of Pineapple. Sprinkle
with brown Sugar, baste with sauce
and brown.

    Gladys B. Smith

126

Mushroom Meat Loaf.

1 lb. ground meat (beef or veal)
1 lb. ham
4 Tbsp. tomato catsup
3 Tsp. green peppers & a little onion
2 eggs slightly beaten
1/2 tsp salt & pepper
1 Can condensed mushroom soup
3/4 Cup dry bread crumbs
1 Can mushrooms.

Add ingredients in order listed with exception of canned mushrooms. Pack half of mixture in greased loaf pan. Press whole mushrooms into centre. Add remaining meal mixture & press whole mushrooms into top layer. Bake 1 hour in moderate oven.
It is well to prepare a few hours before baking.

Plain Meat Loaf.

1 1/2 lbs. ground round steak
1 Cup fine soft bread crumbs
2 eggs
2 Tsp. fine minced onion
1 Cup milk
1 tsp. salt
1/4 tsp. pepper
Mix well and bake in a loaf 1 hour 375°.
Dot with butter or strips of bacon.

Catharine M. Creighton (Mrs. H. A.)

129

HAM LOAF

2 lbs. cured ham,
1½ lbs pork steak,
ground together
2 eggs
1 cup milk
1 cup bread crumbs
Mix all together thoroughly
Add seasonings. Put
in tins and cover
with sauce.
Bake at 350°-400°
for about
1½ hours.
Baste frequently.

Sauce:

1½ cups brown sugar
1 tbsp mustard
½ cup vinegar
½ cup water

Josephine Eisenhower
(Mrs. D. A.)

128

Veal Loaf.

Separate a knuckle of veal in pieces. Wipe, put in kettle with one pound lean veal and one onion. Cover with boiling water and cook slowly until veal is tender. Drain, and chop the meat fine — season with salt and pepper. Garnish bottom of mould with slices of hard boiled egg and parsley. Put in layer of meat, layer of thinly sliced egg, sprinkle with finely chopped parsley and cover with remaining meat. Pour over liquid which should be reduced to one cupful. Press and chill.

J. E. Duff.
(Mrs. William)

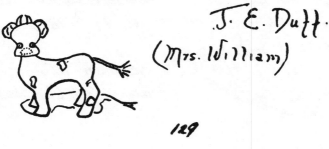

129

Roast Turkey

Select a bird, 6 to 8 months old, with a plump breast. Clean and dry thoroughly. Stuff body cavity lightly and sew opening. Cut off the neck bone, loosen skin over the breast, insert a layer of dressing and sew opening. This flavors and keeps breast meat moist. Wrap thighs in bacon strips, bind thighs and wings firmly to the body. Cover breast and wings with softened butter and sprinkle with flour. Roast, uncovered, breast down, at about 325°, basting with butter and hot water, or with drippings from pan, when needed. Turn to brown breast and sides. Test for completed cooking by inserting a large fork in upper thigh. If no juice comes out bird is cooked. Average cooking time for a 6 to 10 lb. bird is 3 to 3½ hours.

Boscawen Manor
(Frances M. Campbell)

130

Turkey Dressing
(8-10 lb. Bird)

4 cups dry bread crumbs
coarsely ground.
2 tbsps finely chopped onions
1 tsp salt
Sage to taste } Heat brings
Summer savory to taste } out flavor.
½ cup melted butter.
Hot water to moisten.

Summer savory is the main herb
used. Just a suspicion of sage is
needed to round out the flavor

Combine ingredients, adding
water last. Mix lightly with a
fork. If desired, add ½ cup
washed seedless raisins. Do not
stuff the bird too full. The dressing
should be light and fluffy when served.

Boscawen Manor.
(Frances M. Campbell)

Turkey Gravy

Measure drippings in pan. Add ¼ cup flour to ¼ cup drippings. Blend and add liquid — 2 cups of water or stock, or water drained from cooked vegetables — to above amount. Stir quickly to keep from lumping, put through a strainer and set aside to keep hot. Add salt if needed. For giblet gravy add giblets, finely chopped, to completed gravy.

Cranberry Sauce

Add 1 cup of boiling water to 4 cups of cleaned cranberries and cook until soft. Add 2 cups of sugar and bring to a boil. Bottle immediately. This makes a nice firm sauce, attractive for serving, but will not jell if allowed to boil after adding the sugar.

Boscawen Manor
(Frances M. Campbell)

132

Roast Goose

Draw, singe and prepare as for chicken except that pinions (wing tips) are removed. Be sure (as in all fowl) that the preen gland (oil sac) is cut out. Scrub in water with 1 tbsp. of baking soda. Rinse and dry. Stuff with (a) your favorite fowl dressing, heavily seasoned and containing a chopped apple, (b) mashed potatoes, 1 cup chopped onion, salt, pepper and favorite herbs, or (c) peeled, sliced apples and 1 cup of raisins. Place neck, gizzard and heart inside bird with stuffing. Reserve liver for frying. Stitch or skewer openings, tie down wings and leg ends. Rub bird with bacon fat and dust with salt, pepper and ground ginger. Prick skin of breast in many places to let out excess fat. Either place on rack in covered roaster or, if desired, place on a bed of sauerkraut. Roast from 2-4 hours at 350°. Turn frequently and baste often. When breast and legs are tender to touch and the skin is brown and slightly crisp "the goose is cooked." Serve with applesauce seasoned with mace or nutmeg.

Ruth James
135 (Mrs. John F.)

Roast Chicken

1-4 or 5 lb. Chicken
Salt and Pepper
Stuffing and Butter

Clean bird well inside and out. Singe if necessary. Wash thoroughly and wipe dry. Stuff with dressing. Truss and tie. Brush with melted butter, if necessary. Place in oven 325°F. Cook uncovered, breast side up. Keep turning until brown all over. Baste often. Allow 30 minutes per pound.

Dressing

2 Potatoes (Medium)
3 Cups Dry Bread Crumbs
1 Medium Onion
1 Small Apple

3 oz. butter
1 tsp. Salt
1 tsp. Savory
1/4 tsp. Pepper

Boil and mash potatoes. Add bread crumbs. Put small piece butter in frying pan, melt, add chopped onion and apple. Cover and let simmer till done. Add remainder butter. Combine all ingredients. and mix well.

Violet D. Allen
(Mrs. L. Allen)

CHICKEN SUPREME

Joint a 3 or 4 lb. fowl. Cover with water. Cook until tender. Remove skin and bone.

Add –
- 1 can sieved tomatoes
- 1 can mushrooms
- 1 can lima beans
- 1 c. diced carrots
- 1 c. diced celery
- Salt and pepper

Simmer 1 hr. and stir occasionally. Serve with toast or boiled rice. This should be cooked in a heavy bottom pot.

Evelyn V. B. Ritcey
(Mrs C. B.)

135

Fricasse Chicken

Boil fowl, either whole or in large pieces, with salt and a large onion in water sufficient to cover, until tender. (Test with fork.)

Drain — roll large pieces in flour and salt and sauté lightly in either chicken fat or butter..

Thicken with flour and flavor with celery salt.

Belle Backman Mack
(Mrs. S. E. Mack.)

136

Southern Fried Chicken

Clean chicken and cut in serving
pieces. Roll in flour
seasoned with salt
and pepper; brown
on both sides in $\frac{1}{2}$ cup very hot fat.
Reduce heat and cook slowly, about 1
hour, turning pieces to brown evenly on
all sides or finish cooking in mod.
slow oven (325°). Make cream gravy
from 1/4 cup of the pan drippings.

Libby Taylor
(Mrs. R.C.)

137

Chicken Pie

3 cups cooked chicken
12 small cooked white onions
1 cup well seasoned chicken broth
1 cup cooked sliced carrots
Baking powder biscuit dough
4 tbsp. flour
6 tbsp. water

Arrange chicken, onions and carrots in casserole. Heat chicken broth with flour to thicken. Pour over chicken. Make biscuit dough and cut into rings. Arrange on chicken and bake in hot oven.

Golden Sauce

1 cup milk
1 cup chicken broth
2 tbsp. butter
2 tbsp. flour

salt
¼ tsp. pepper
1 egg yolk
1 tsp. lemon juice

Melt butter, add flour when bubbling, stir in milk and chicken broth gradually. Add pepper and salt as needed. Just before removing from fire add egg yolk beaten and lemon juice stirring rapidly.

B. Jean Morrow (Mrs. C. J.)

Chicken Cacciatora

4 lb. chicken (cut in serving pieces)

½ c. flour	3 sprigs parsley
1 tsp. salt	1 bay leaf
½ c. fat	4 c. tomatoes
¼ c. chopped onion	1 tsp. salt
1 garlic clove (grated fine)	pepper
¼ c. chopped carrot	

Dredge chicken in flour, sprinkle with salt and brown in fat until golden on all sides. Place in covered dish in warm place. Brown onion, garlic, carrot, parsley and bay leaf in fat left in pan.

Strain tomatoes. (You should have 2 c. pulp. Add tomato pulp to browned vegetables in frying pan, add 1 tsp. salt and a dash of pepper, and bring to a boil. Add chicken and simmer 30 min. or until chicken is tender.

Verna D. Smith
(Mrs. Russell G.)

139

Creamed Chicken

6 tbsp. butter
6 tbsp. flour
1½ cups milk
1 tsp. salt
1 egg yolk
4 cups diced chicken
1 cup diced celery
1½ cups chicken stock
1 small can pimento
pepper and paprika

Melt butter in double boiler, add flour, salt & pepper. Blend. Add warmed milk and chicken stock and stir constantly till thick. Cover and cook 20 minutes. Add paprika, pimento, chicken & celery. Last of all add the slightly beaten egg yolk. This may be served in pastry shells or on toast if desired. Serves 12 - 15.

Edythe E. Oxner
(Mrs. J. W.)

Chicken Ring Mould

Have a four pound chicken ready as for roasting. Put into a deep kettle and cover with water, adding one onion, one carrot and a few celery leaves. Season with salt and pepper. Cook until the chicken is tender, take from liquor and strain. Let cool also let the liquor it was cooked in cool after you have strained it. Skim off all fat. Then reduse (by cooking) the stock to two cupfuls. Add one tablespoon gelatine softened in a little cold water. Take the chicken meat from bones, removing skin and gristle. Chop meat fine. Season to taste, then mixe chopped chicken with the rest of the slightly thickened jelly. Pack into mould. Chill before serving

Dorothy Mosher
(Mrs. P. 31)

143

B.A.J.

= Roast Black Duck =

The wild duck should be cleaned and hung up 3 or 4 days.

Save the giblets and toe: with the neck simmer in water with onion, pepper & salt for a gravy.

Put apple, carrot or onion in each bird to draw the strong flavor (not to be eaten) Pepper and salt them and lay strip of clear salt pork on each breast. Little water in pan. Bake in med: hot oven 1 3/4 to 2 hours. Baste & turn.

Thicken the giblet broth with flour and add some fat from pan.

Make separate dressing if required & dont forget the cranberries. — Lillian Mosher (Mrs Stephen)

142

———— Rabbit Pie ————

2 rabbits
1/4 lb. fat pork
4 eggs
pepper

butter
little powdered mace
lemon juice
puff paste

Cut rabbits into ten pieces. Soak in salt and water half an hour and simmer until half done, in enough water to cover. Cut pork in slices and boil eggs hard. Lay some pork in bottom of dish and next a layer of rabbit upon this spread slices of egg, pepper and butter. Sprinkle with mace, a few drops of lemon juice upon each piece of meat. Proceed in this manner until dish is full – top layer being pork. Pour in water in which rabbit was boiled; when you have salted it and added a few lumps of butter rolled in flour, cover with puff paste. Make a hole in the middle. Bake 1 hour. Cover with paper if it should boil too fast.

Jean B. Burke
(Mrs. Archie)

145

A Curry.

A curry is never that vile travesty, — a cream sauce disgustingly tinted with curry powder!

There is considerable, permissible variation in preparation and extra ingredients, but basically for 2½ lbs. of meat, fowl or fish proceed as follows: Melt 4 tbsp. butter in pan, sauté therein, 2 large chopped onions, add 1½ tbsp. Madras curry powder, ½ tsp. savoury herbs and stir with a ~~wooden~~ ~~spoon~~ for 2 min. Add 1 pt. of appropriate stock and/or coconut milk, 1 handful of raisins, 1 chopped clove of garlic, 1 large chopped, peeled apple, ½ tsp. black pepper, ½ tsp. ground ginger, salt to taste and juice of half a lemon. Cook slowly 10 min. Cut uncooked meat etc. in 1 inch pieces, dredge in flour, fry in butter, then add to above sauce (leftovers may be used. Fowl meat should be freed from bone.) Simmer gently for ½ hr. (fish 5 min.) Adjust to taste and smell. It should be a smooth blend of sweet and sour, salt and spice, together with a hot meaty fragrance and of thin but not watery consistency. The true lover will demand ~~extra~~ cayenne and ginger that the sweat may stand upon the forehead. Pieces of cucumber, eggplant, Tomato, etc. maybe cooked in a curry, ~~but~~ ~~never~~ ~~potatoes~~ ~~nor~~ ~~flour~~ ~~for~~ ~~thickening~~. Serve with fluffy boiled Patna rice: First place rice on each plate, then in a central well heap the curry. Pour extra liquid over rice. Pass sweet, hot, gingery Chutney and any or all of the following to be added by the individual if desired — Bombay duck (a smelly, dried fish), crisp bits of fried, smoked or cured fish, dried shrimps, chopped hard-boiled egg, fresh, grated coconut, chopped outer peel of citrus fruits, chopped sweet or hot peppers, chopped roasted almonds or cashews, chopped raw onions or fried onion rings, etc.

Provide a dessert spoon (quite correct!) as well as knife and fork — and don't forget the cooling drinks!

Mary S. James.
"Tower Hill" L'burg.

144

Vegetable AND Supper Dishes

145

CHOP SUEY

1 cup cooked macaroni

1 lb. hamburg

3 or 4 medium size onions

½ can tomato soup

½ can tomatoes

salt and pepper

Fry hamburg. When it is slightly brown push it to one side of pan and gently fry onions. Arrange in casserole, one layer macaroni; the meat and onions, then another layer of macaroni. Pour tomato soup and tomatoes over mixture. Over top sprinkle plain or buttered cracker crumbs. Bake 20 to 30 min. at 325°F.

Christabel Cantelope
(Mrs. J.C.)

146

BEEF GOULASH

Dice $\frac{1}{4}$ lb. fat (salt pork)
Fry it with 2 medium
sized onions, minced, until
golden brown. Place in deep
casserole and cover with 4 large
potatoes, and 4 large carrots, cut in
quarters. Add next 1 lb. Round steak,
which has been cut in small squares, 2",
Rolled slightly in salted flour. Pour
over this 1 can tomato juice (soup) and
equal amount of water, which has
been seasoned with 1 tsp salt
$\frac{1}{8}$ tsp. Pepper
$\frac{1}{4}$ tsp. celery salt.

Bake $2\frac{1}{2}$ hrs.

Mildred Adams Riker
(Mrs. F. F.)
147

Dinner in a dish.

4 Tablespoons Crisco
1 Sliced Onion.
1 lb Hamburger.
1 Green Pepper.
2 Eggs.
1 can Tomatoes.
1 can Whole Kernel Corn.
Bread crumbs.

Fry onion & green pepper in Crisco
3 mins low heat add meat & 1 tsp
salt. Sear meat until grey, take off
stove & break in eggs. Mix all & put
in baking dish, layer of corn, layer
of meat, layer of tomatoes until all
are used up. Sprinkle with bread crumbs.
Bake ½ hr in oven 375°

G. Van der Seual
(née D.C.)

148

LAMB BARBECUE

2 cups cold roast lamb cut in small pieces
2 tbsp. butter
1 small onion
¾ cup diced celery
¾ tsp. dry mustard
2 tbsp. brown sugar
1½ tsp. salt
¾ tsp. chili powder
3 tbsp. vinegar
1½ cup tomato juice
½ cup water

Lightly brown onion and celery in fat. Add dry
ingredients. Add vinegar, tomato juice and
water. Simmer 20 minutes. Add lamb and
simmer slowly for 40 minutes more, or until
the sauce has thickened and flavored
lamb. Heating the lamb slowly in this tasty
rich barbecue sauce permits the meat
to take on a new flavor. Serve in a
ring of lima beans or peas. This is a good
way to vary left over lamb.

May Eisenhauer
(Mrs D.M.)

149

LUNCHEON CASSEROLE

Melt 6 tbsp. of butter in a heavy double saucepan. Add 5 tbsp of flour and cook and stir until mixture bubbles. Add 1½ cups of chicken stock and 1 cup of top milk and stir until the sauce is smooth and thickened. Season with salt.

Combine 1 cup of cooked asparagus, ½ lb. of sliced fresh mushrooms that have been sauteed for about 10 min. in a small amt. of butter, 2 cups of cooked macaroni, cut into inch lengths, and 3 hard boiled eggs, chopped. Combine with the sauce and pour into a well buttered casserole. Top with ½ cup of grated American cheese and and bake in a 350° oven for 25 to 30 min.

Vivian P. Zinck
(Mrs. R.C.)

Roast Beef Hash

7 medium potatoes pared + sliced
2 tbsp fat
1½ cups roast beef cut bite size
1½ " roast beef gravy

Melt fat in heavy pan add
potatoes fry slowly about 15 min
turn several times add beef + gravy
simmer untill potatoes are well
done salt + pepper to taste

Frances Himmelman
(Mrs H.B.)

Hot Salmon Dish

Put in baking dish
one large tin of
salmon (drained).
Spread with bread
crumbs and dot with butter, pepper
and salt. Pour over this about 1/2 cup
milk. Bake 1/2 hr. in hot oven.
Serve with creamed potatoes and peas.

Alice Y. Burke
(Mrs. Dougald)

Tuna Dish

1 Can Tuna Fish
1 Potato   1 Carrot
2 sticks Celery
1/2 can Peas
Salt & Pepper.

Method: Cook diced raw vegetables in
small amount of water. Make a white
sauce, using water in which vegetables
were cooked, along with some milk. Put
Tuna Fish, cooked vegetables and peas in
casserole, add white sauce and mix
together. Cover with rich biscuit dough
and bake one half hour in hot oven.

Alice Y. Burke
(Mrs. Dougald)

152

Tuna Fish with Cheese Roll Crust

2 slices onion   3 tbsp. butter
6 tbsp. flour   1 tsp. salt
½ c. sweet green peppers, diced
3 c. milk   1 tbsp. lemon juice
1 lge can tuna fish.

     Melt butter, add peppers and onion, cook until soft. Add flour, blend well. Add salt, milk, stir until thick and smooth. Boil 2 mins.. Add remaining ingredients. Put in large baking dish. Cover with Cheese rolls.

Cheese Rolls

1½ c flour   3 tsp. baking powder
½ tsp. salt   ½ c. milk
3 tbsp. shortening   ¾ c. grated cheese
Few grains cayenne   2 pimentos, chopped

     Sift together flour, baking powder, salt and cayenne. Add shortening. Mix as for Baking Powder Biscuits. Roll out in sheet 8 x 12. Sprinkle with grated cheese and pimento. Roll like jelly roll. Cut in slices. Place on top of creamed mixture in baking dish.
     Bake in hot oven for 30 minutes.

Jean C. Rafuse
(Mrs. E. W.)

Salmon dish with Cucumber Sauce.

1/2 tsp. salt
1 1/2 tbsp. sugar.
1/2 tbsp. flour.
1 tsp. mustard
2 egg yolks
3/4 c. milk
1/4 c. vinegar
3/4 tbsp. gelatine
soaked in 2 tbsp. c. water
method: mix and boil dressing, add gelatine and when cold mix in one large can salmon (celery, green pepper or peas may be added). put in mold, chill, cut in slices, serve on lettuce with cucumber sauce.

Cucumber Sauce

1/2 c. whipped cream
1/4 tsp Salt.
2 tbsp. vinegar.
1 chopped cucumber.

Hilda Fr. Young
(Mrs. D. E.)

SHIPYARDS SCENE

SALMON ROLL.

2 cups flour
4 tsp. Baking pdr
½ tsp. salt
4 tbsp. Shortening (or butter)
⅔ cup milk (approx.)
1 lb tin salmon
4 Tbsp. top milk or light cream
2 tbsp lemon juice

Make biscuit dough with first five ingredients
Roll out on bread board (¼" thick)
Spread the minced salmon (which has
been mixed with lemon juice and cream and
seasoned to taste) over the biscuit dough.
Roll (as jelley roll), cut in slices —
place in large sized muffin tins
and bake in 400° oven
Serve hot with hot egg sauce —
— white sauce with chopped hard-
boiled eggs added to it — add a little
chopped parsley.

Georgie M. Mason (Mrs. H.F.)

156

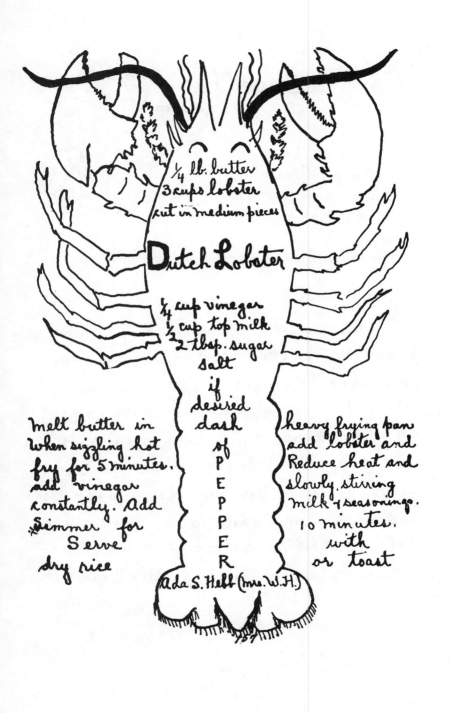

¼ lb. butter
3 cups lobster
cut in medium pieces

Dutch Lobster

¼ cup vinegar
½ cup top milk
2 tbsp. sugar
salt
if
desired
dash
of
P
E
P
P
E
R

melt butter in ... heavy frying pan
when sizzling hot ... add lobster and
fry for 5 minutes. ... Reduce heat and
add vinegar ... slowly stirring
constantly. Add ... milk & seasonings.
Simmer for ... 10 minutes.
Serve ... with
dry rice ... or toast

Ada S. Hebb (Mrs. W.H.)

Corn Souffle

3 Tbsp butter
2 Tbsp. flour
1½ cup milk
1 can corn
3 eggs
salt and pepper.

Start making cream sauce by
blending butter and flour in saucepan over low heat, add the milk,
which has been heated, stirring
as it thickens, add corn, and salt
and pepper to taste, then the egg
yolks, slightly beaten. Put in oven (350°)
and bake until thick, (as custard), then
fold in stiffly beaten egg whites,
return to oven until slightly brown.

Georgie Mason.
(Mrs H. F.)

158

Corn Scallop

2 cups corn

1 cup cracker dust

2 eggs

1½ cups milk

butter - size walnut

½ cup grated cheese

Beat eggs well and put in
dish with corn, milk and melted
butter. Put cracker dust and
cheese on top of casserole
with dash of paprika. Bake
thirty minutes.

Ada L. Tanner
(Mrs. G. P.)

159

Macaroni, Cheese, Tomatoes

Cook 1c. macaroni as
directed on package, till water is
all absorbed. Stir in 1½ c. grated
cheese, 1 can tomatoes, salt, pepper
to taste. Turn into casserole,
sprinkle with cheese & dots of
butter. Bake 40 min 300°

Ethel F. Mosher.
(Mrs Daniel)

160

Fluffy Egg Omelette

Separate yolks and whites of 3 or 4 eggs. Beat yolks very light and add 1 tbsp. milk for each egg. Season with salt and pepper.

Beat whites till stiff but not dry, and fold carefully into yolks.

Melt a little butter in frying pan, to grease all over. When hot, pour in the mixture, spreading evenly.

Lower heat, and cook over low heat till set. Fold and serve.

Before folding, an omelette may be "packed", that is — some flavorful hot addition may be spread over half of it, before other half is folded over, such as :

Chopped ham or bacon.

Creamed chicken or ham. or

Diced veal in tomato sauce.   sauce may be poured around omelette if desired.

Lillian E. Thurlow
(Mrs S. L.)

161

-Escalloped Eggs with Cheese-

3 T. butter
¼ c. flour
1 t. salt
2 c. milk
grated onion

¾ c. grated cheese
(Can. cheddar)
1 c. buttered
bread crumbs
6. hard cooked eggs

Melt butter in saucepan
Add flour, salt, onion, and
milk gradually, stirring.
Cook until thickened.
Stir in cheese.
Slice eggs and add to sauce.
Arrange in casserole,
topping with crumbs.
Bake about 20 mts.

Dorothy B. Crouse
(Mrs. C. Q.)

162

Potato Scallop

6 medium sized potatos or
enough to fill casserole
Butter size of small egg,
1 onion, salt, milk.
Slice potatos thinly put layer
in casserole then part of
onion, salt, and bits of butter
alternately till casserole is
filled leaving some butter
for top. Fill dish 3/4 full
with milk sprinkle with
dried bread crumbs. Bake
1 hour or until potatos are done.

Stella a Lohnes
(Mo Ja)

Stuffed Potato Surprise

Bake six potatoes and cut a thin, lengthwise slice from the side of each. Scoop out pulp without breaking shell, mash and season to taste with salt and pepper. Add three-fourths of a cup of hot milk, six tablespoons of shortening, eight minced stuffed olives, two tablespoons of chopped green pepper and a cup of chopped, left-over meat. Mix thoroughly, refill shells, brush top with milk, return to hot oven to reheat and brown. Serves six.

B. Jean Morrow
(Mrs. C. J.)

164

Candied Sweet Potato

¾ cup orange juice
½ tsp. grated orange rind
1 cup water
½ cup sugar
3 tbsp. light corn syrup
¼ tsp. salt
3 tbsp. butter
6 sweet potatoes or yams

Peel sweet potatoes and cut in half, lengthwise. Combine orange juice, rind, water, sugar, corn syrup, salt and butter, and pour over sweet potatoes arranged in a casserole or baking dish. Bake covered in a moderate oven until tender, 30 or 40 minutes. Baste occasionally. Remove lid last 10 minutes to brown.

Variation:
Just before removing from oven, add a layer of marshmallows and brown

B. Jean Morrow
(Mrs. C.J.)

165

— Scalloped Tomato and Onion —

1 can tomato
2 cups sliced onions
buttered bread crumbs
salt
pepper
1 T. butter

Parboil onions 15 mts., drain
Put layers of tomatoes
and onions in baking dish.
Sprinkle with salt and
pepper.
Cover with crumbs.
Bake until onions are soft
and top brown ———
about 30 mts.

Dorothy B. Crouse.
(Mrs. G. G.)

166

Baked Onions with Cheese

Boil two cups onions until tender -

Make a sauce of -

    2 tbsp. butter
    2 tbsp. flour.
    ½ tsp. salt.
    ½ tsp. pepper
    1 cup. rich milk.

When hot add ½ cup. of grated nippy cheese.

Top. with bread crumbs and bake in a moderate oven until brown.

(Mrs. W. P.) Mildred P. Potter

Cabbage & Cheese Casserole.

½ head Cabbage - Shredded.
2 cups White Sauce.
1 cup grated Cheese. (sharp)

Boil shredded cabbage in salted water 20 minutes. Drain.
Grease casserole, put in layer of cabbage, layer of white sauce, layer of cheese. Repeat until all is used.

Bake at 375° for 30 minutes

K. Heckman.

= Dandelion Greens =

Dig up the plants, whole,
in early spring before the
buds have opened. Remove
the brown leaves
and trim off
the roots. Wash
in several waters.
Put on to cook in
salted water and
when it boils add
a pinch of soda. When done
drain well and pour the fat
from fried salt pork, ham
or bacon over it.

Vinegar is added to suit
the individual taste.

Dandelions are a natural
spring tonic. Lillian Mosher
(Mrs Stephen)

169

Corn Fritters

Beat two egg yolks.
Add one can creamed corn,
one tsp. salt, one cup all
purpose flour, one tsp. B.P.

Mix well: fold in
stiffly beaten egg whites.
Drop from top of spoon
into hot fat (deep lard).

When cooking turn
frequently. When well brown,
drain.

Serve with maple syrup,
corn syrup or molasses.

Muriel M. Y. Zinck
(Mrs. K. D.)

Waffles

2 cups flour,
1 teaspoon salt,
1 tablespoon sugar.
3 teaspoons baking powder,
2 cups milk,
2 eggs beat separately,
4 tablespoons butter,
Sift flour, salt, sugar,
and baking powder,
Add milk and butter
and the eggs to mixture.
Serve with — corn or maple syrup.
Put four or five tablespoons of
batter into waffle iron.

Pan Cakes.

3 eggs, 1 cup milk,
1 teaspoon soda,
pinch of salt, flour
enough to make a stiff
batter, serve with — corn
or maple syrup.

Mary C. Ryner.

(Mrs. S. W.)

191

White Sauce.

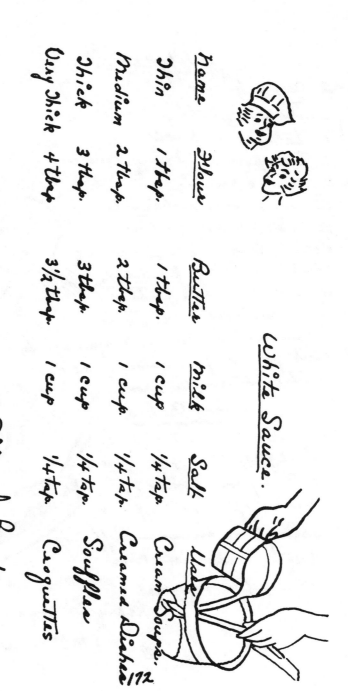

Name	Flour	Butter	Milk	Salt	Use
Thin	1 tbsp.	1 tbsp.	1 cup	¼ tsp.	Cream Soups.
Medium	2 tbsp.	2 tbsp.	1 cup.	¼ tsp.	Creamed Dishes 172
Thick	3 tbsp.	3 tbsp.	1 cup	¼ tsp.	Soufflés
Very Thick	4 tbsp.	3½ tbsp.	1 cup	¼ tsp.	Croquettes

Alice J. Burke
(Mrs. Dougald)

SALADS
and Dressings

BACKMAN

173

Frozen Fruit Pudding

½ lb Marshmallows each one cut in 4 pieces. 1c cherries cut in halves, 1C Sliced or cubed pineapple drained and cut in pieces.

To marshmallows add 1c miracle whip, Cherries and pineapple. Fold 1c. cream which has been whipped Put in Frig. and freeze at ordinary temperature for 4 hours.

Serve on lettuce.

Mildred Walters
(Mrs Angus)

Emerald Salad

1 pkg. Lime Jello—
dissolve in 1 cup
hot pineapple juice.
Let set until fairly
stiff.

Add—
2/3 cup chopped celery
2/3 cup chopped apples
2/3 cup chopped pineapple
1/2 cup whipped cream
1/2 cup mayonnaise

Mayonnaise Dressing

1 cup milk (heat over hot water) add
3 beaten eggs.
In another sauce pan heat 3/4 cup
vinegar.
In a bowl put 2 table flour, 2
tbsp butter, 6 tbsp sugar, 3/4 tsp
mustard. Mix together. Add milk
to make it pour. Cook until
thick. Add vinegar.

Lorna Oxner

PARTY SALAD

Drain 1 can No.2 crushed pineapple. Add 1 cup boiling water to the juice, and 1 pkg. lemon jello. While hot add 6 oz. of Philadelphia cream cheese. Stir until well dissolved, then put aside to cool. Whip ½ pt. heavy cream, fold it into the jello mixture. Then add crushed pineapple, ¼ cup of carrots, ½ cup celery, ¼ cup green pepper, ⅓ cup walnuts, all diced fine.

Vivian P. Zinck
(Mrs. R. C.)

30 MINUTE SALAD

2 tbsp. gelatin

1 pt. boiling water

3 pimentos

2 pkgs. lemon jello

1 can crushed pineapple

2 pkgs. cream cheese

1 orange (sliced)

Soak plain gelatin in a little cold water. Add boiling water to jello, stir both together. Let stand 30 minutes. Add pineapple and pimento cut fine. Work cheese until creamy, add to gelatin mixture. Beat until stiff. Let stand 8 hours or longer. Garnish with slices of orange around entire mould. If possible use ring mould. Serve with the following cream dressing.

CREAM DRESSING

3 tbsp. cream

few drops lemon juice

1 cup mayonnaise

May Eisenhauer
(Mrs. D.M.)

177

Tomato Aspic

3½ T. gelatin   ½ T. salt
4 T. sugar   3 C. tomato juice
3 T. vinegar off sweet pickles 1 C. consomme.

Sprinkle gelatin on one cup of cold
tomato juice; add salt, sugar and
consomme to remainder of tomato
juice. Heat and add to softened
gelatin; add vinegar. Pour into
mold & stir occasionally until
mixture begins to thick

Anne Maycock (Mrs. N.T.)

178

Tuna, Crab or Salmon Salad.

1 envelope gelatine soaked in ¼ c. cold water
1 c. fish
½ c. chopped celery
½ c. green pepper, chopped
2 tbsp. green olives, chopped
¾ c. salad dressing
½ tsp. salt
1 tbsp. vinegar
Dash paprika

Soak gelatine in cold water, then dissolve in ¼ c. boiling water. Add ingredients. Pour into moulds soaked in cold water.

Verna D. Smith
(Mrs. Russell G.)

179

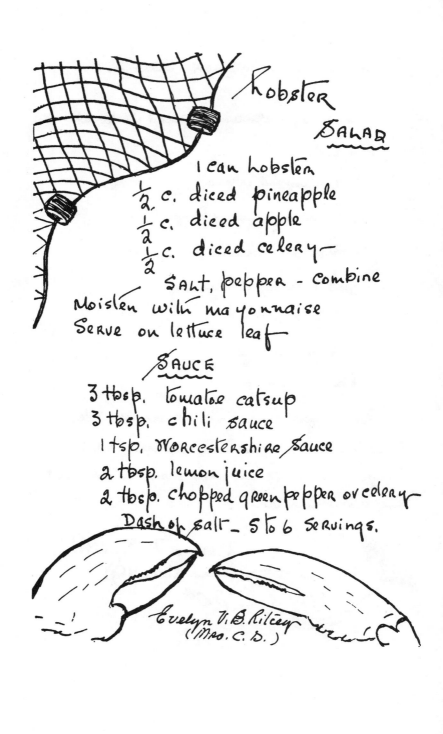

Lobster
Salad

1 can lobster
½ c. diced pineapple
½ c. diced apple
½ c. diced celery —
salt, pepper - combine
Moisten with mayonnaise
Serve on lettuce leaf

Sauce

3 tbsp. tomatoe catsup
3 tbsp. chili sauce
1 tsp. Worcestershire sauce
2 tbsp. lemon juice
2 tbsp. chopped green pepper or celery
Dash of salt — 5 to 6 servings.

Evelyn V. B. Ritcey
(Mrs. C. D.)

Sea Food Picnic Salad

2 cups flaked
cooked or canned
fish.
$\frac{1}{2}$ tsp salt
$\frac{1}{8}$ tsp. pepper.
1 cup cooked diced
potatoes.
$\frac{1}{2}$ cup chopped onions
1 cup chopped celery
$\frac{1}{2}$ cup chopped green
pepper.
$\frac{1}{2}$ cup salad dressing.

To flaked fish add salt,
pepper, potatoes, onions,
celery, green pepper and mix
well. Fold in salad dressing.
Serve on crisp lettuce.

Dorothy Mosher
(Mrs. P. H.)

181

Chicken Mousse

2 cups ground cooked chicken
½ cup salad dressing
2 tbls. lemon juice
¾ cup minced celery
¾ cup heavy cream whipped
    salt and pepper
1½ tbls. gelatine
½ cup cold chicken stock

Blend chicken, salad dressing
lemon juice and celery,
Fold in the whipped cream,
Season to taste, Fold in the
gelatine which has been softened
in the cold chicken stock, dissolved
over hot water, then cooled
Pour into mould and chill until firm
Serve on lettuce cups.

Sadie C. Krickle
(Mrs J. R.)

Jellied Ham and Celery Salad

Dissolve one package lime jelly in 1 ¾ cups boiling water. Add ¼ cup vinegar, ½ tsp. salt. Chill.

When thickening folds in.
1 cup chopped ham.
1½ cup chopped celery
1 tbsp. chopped onion
2 sweet pickles, chopped fine

Pour into individual moulds. Chill Serve on lettuce leaf. Garnish with sliced tomatoes.

Phoebe C. Conrad
(Mrs. R. D.)

183

— Potato Salad — (Hot)

Cook the potatoes and cube or slice them while hot. Put 1 c. sour cream, ½ tsp chopped onion, 2 tbsp vinegar, 3/4 tsp sugar, pepper & salt in a frying pan. Simmer a few minutes. Combine with the potatoes and 1 or 2 sliced hard boiled eggs.

Served on lettuce leaves, garnished with tomatoes, radishes _etc_ makes this simple salad attractive and appetizing.

Ethel F. Mosler.
(Mrs. Daniel)

184

Tossed Salad

Cut fine 1/2 head lettuce, about 3 inches cucumber, 1 stick celery, 1 tbsp. onion, few rings of green or red pepper, 1/2 tomato sliced. Add salt and pepper to taste. Mix together and keep cold until ready to serve. This is best with a French dressing.

Agnes P. Sweeny
(Mrs. D. L.)

THE GREAT
CELERI
TUMBLING
ACT

Cabbage Salad

2 cups finely shredded cabbage
1 cup heavy cream
¼ cup vinegar
2 tbsp sugar
½ teasp salt
½ teasp celery seed
½ teasp mustard seed

Mix all together + stir
untill quite foamy

Frances Himmelman
(Mrs H.B.)

LUNENBURG'S MEMORIAL
TO HER DEAD OF WORLD WAR II
1939 ～ 1945

187

Chicken Salad

2 cups diced chicken
½ cup chopped celery
¼ cup drained crushed
         pineapple (optional)
pepper and salt to taste

Combine ingredients with
mayonnaise. Toss lightly and
serve in lettuce cups.

Boiled Dressing or Mayonnaise

4 beaten eggs   6 tbsp sugar
6 tbsp. flour   4 tbsp butter
2 cups hot water   4 tsp. mustard
1 cup vinegar   2 tsp salt
         dash of paprika

Cook in double boiler until
thick. Thin with cream when
using.

Hazel Hopgood (Mrs. R. St. C.)

188

FRENCH DRESSING
" ——— "

1 pint vinegar
¼ cup tarragon vinegar
½ " salad oil
⅔ " sugar
2 tsp. salt
½ " pepper
2 " grated horseradish
1 " dry mustard
1 " paprika
1 " worcestershire sauce
½ clove garlic minced fine or dash garlic powder
⅓ btl tomato chutney or ketchup
5 drops Tabasco sauce
1 small onion sliced

——— " ——— "

Put all ingredients into a large bottle and shake thoroughly until blended. The above amounts are approximate, and may be varied to suit individual tastes.

A small amount of this dressing added to regular Mayonnaise will give an extra filip to Meat. Fish or Vegetable salads.

M. Pearl Oliver
(Mrs. B. G.)

189

PRETTY FANCIES in SANDWICHES

ROLL UPS For party sandwiches, trim crusts from fresh bread slices. Lay asparagus tip across one end of each. Roll up. Serve whole or cut in halves with a bit of parsley tucked in one or both ends; if desired.

OPEN FACE Make open face in stars, circles and diamonds. You can use any of four fancy cookie cutters for intriguing shapes. The round sandwich is spread with mayonnaise, sports a tomatoe slice and is topped by a dab of mayonnaise and a tiny sprig of parsley.

The diamond shape is covered with creamy chopped egg filling and garnished with three crisp radish slices. For the star-shaped sandwiches spread with creamy cheese; garnish with slices of stuffed olives, while the tips of the others can be dipped in finely chopped parsley or spread with minced ham and pickle.

PINWHEELS are EASY

For pin wheels, Trim the crust from a loaf of fresh bread and cut lengthwise slices. Then spread with butter and filling of minced ham and roll around whole gerkins or olives at one end. Next roll as for jelly roll; butter the end and press it against the roll; wrap and chill.

CHECKER BOARDS Put alternate slices of brown and white bread together with cream cheese to make ribbon sandwiches. For checker boards pile ribbon slices so that each brown stripe lies directly over a white one. For filling creamy cheese, (plain or pimento) is best.

TOASTED BACON

Easy to eat - fun to fix

Bacon Cylinders - (hot from the oven): Remove crusts from thin slices buttered sandwich bread. Place one very thin slice of cheese on each bread slice. Roll up "jelly roll fashion", and skewer with toothpicks. Tie, in single knot, with $\frac{1}{2}$" wide bacon strips. Wrap in damp cloth and chill. To serve, bake on rack in hot oven (400°) about 8 minutes, or till bacon is cooked.

CALLA LILIES

For calla lilies, fold opposite corners, cornucopia - fashion, over an asparagus tip. Press over lapping edges together firmly.

191

INDIVIDUAL SANDWICH LOAVES

Next time its your turn to entertain just make these party treats. For each small sandwich loaf; butter a slice of bread; spread with chicken filling. Top with a second slice of bread, buttered on both sides; spread with egg filling. Top with a third slice of bread, buttered on both sides; spread with ham filling. Cover with a fourth slice, buttered side down. Mash the cream cheese in a bowl; moisten with cream; beat until fluffy. Frost the top and sides with cheese. Garnish with sliced stuffed olives, parsley, these miniature replicas of the large sandwich loaf.

For this glamorous party sandwich loaf an oblong loaf of bread is used. Spread six slices of bread with yummy mixtures of various kinds _ cheese spread, chicken salad mixture, tomato slices, ham, and egg salad. Garnish this cream cheese covered loaf as prettily as your artistic talents permit. Stuffed olive slices, radish roses, green pepper bits are easy.

CLUB SANDWICH

Toast and butter three slices of white bread. Arrange lettuce, sliced chicken, crisp bacon and sliced tomato on one piece of toast. Spread with a highly seasoned mayonnaise. Cover with a second piece of toast and repeat the process. Cut in triangles. Garnish with lettuce, pickles and stuffed olives.

Mildred Adams Pilcher
192   (Mrs. E. E.)

Pies and pastries

Pastry

2 cups pastry flour

⅔ cup crisco

2 tbsp. butter

½ tsp. salt

⅓ cup ice cold water

Blend flour , crisco , butter , salt well with pastry blender. Add water gradually. This is sufficient pastry for two pie shells or 1 covered pie

Ada L. Tanner

(Mrs. G. P.)

Apple Pie

6 tart apples   ½ tsp. salt
1 cup sugar   1 tbsp. butter
½ tsp. nutmeg   2 tsp. lemon juice
or cinnamon   Few gratings lemon rind

Line a 9 inch pie plate with pastry.
Pare and cut apples in quarters, then
thin slices. Put alternate layers of
apples and mixture of sugar, spices
lemon juice & rind until plate is filled.
Dot over with butter. Moisten edge of crust
with ice water, cover with top crust
with slits in it and press edges together.
Bake in oven 425° F. for 15 minutes,
reduce temperature to 350° F. for 40 minutes.

Deep Apple Pie

Prepare apples same way as
for apple pie. Arrange in deep
baking dish. Cover with same mixture of brown
sugar, spices, lemon juice and rind. Dot over with butter.
Cover with pastry, cut the size of the dish and press
it down around edges. With tines of fork mark pastry
in 6 squares, making a slit in center of each square.
Bake in oven 425°F. for 20 min. and reduce to 350°F.
for 30 - 40 min. longer. Take from oven and pour ½ cup
cream in each slit in pastry square. Serve warm.

Joyce L. Tupper (Mrs. J. A.)

195

Fruit Pies

Line 10 inch pie plate with pastry. Mix 1/2 to 3/4 cup sugar according to taste and 1 T. minute tapioca with any of the following fruit. Strawberries, raspberries, blackberries, blueberries or huckleberries. Cover with pastry and flute edges. Brush with butter. Bake 45 minutes. Bake at 425°F for 20 minutes, then reduce heat to 375° F.

Lois J. Himmelman
(Mrs Thomas)

Custard Pie.

3 eggs
1/2 cup sugar
2 " milk
1/4 tsp. salt
1/4 tsp. vanilla or nutmeg.

Beat eggs slightly add sugar
and salt, milk and
flavoring. Pour into a pie
plate lined with pastry.
Bake until firm.

Lillie M Deal
(Mrs J. W.)

197

Pumpkin or Squash Pie

1 cup Pumpkin or Squash
½ cup. brown Sugar
2 tbsp. molasses
1 tbsp. butter (melted)
1 tbsp. cinnamon.
½ tsp. ginger.
½ tsp. salt.
2 eggs.
1 cup. top milk.
1 tsp. lemon.

Add sugar, molasses, spices, salt and melted
butter, to pumpkin or squash. Beat eggs
slightly and add. Then add milk and mix
thoroughly. Bake in pie shell in oven
475° for ten minutes, then in 325° for
45° minutes. Garnish with whipped cream.

Flo. E. Powers.

198   (Mrs. A.F.)

Lemon Pie Filling

1 cup boiling water
1 tbsp. butter
1 lemon
4 eggs
3/4 cup sugar
3 tsps. cornstarch.

Meringue.

4 egg whites
3 tbsps. sugar
1 tsp. lemon juice.

Put in double boiler the boiling water & butter. Wash lemon, grate the rind, adding this to water & butter. Squeeze 4 tbsps lemon juice into a cup. Separate eggs, beating whites & yolks separately. Add to yolks, sugar thoroughly mixed with cornstarch. Add lemon juice and beat well. Add this mixture to the boiling water, rind & butter. Stir until thickened. Beat egg whites until stiff and separate into two parts, adding one portion to lemon mixture and fold in carefully. Pour this into baked 9" pie shell.

Meringue.

To the remaining egg whites add sugar & lemon juice & beat well. Pile on pie, sealing edges & brown.

Evelyn V. Zinck
(Mrs. B. E.)

199

Rhubarb Custard Pie Filling

2 c. rhubarb   1 tbsp. butter
3   eggs   1 tbsp cornstarch
1 c. sugar

Cook rhubarb in top part of double boiler. Mix sugar and cornstarch together, add to rhubarb cook until creamy. Add butter, pour over beaten egg yolks. Return to double boiler, cook just enough to thicken egg yolks. Cool; pour into baked pie shell.

Make meringue from egg whites, put on top and bake until light brown.

Jean C. Rafuse
(Mrs. E. W.)

200

Banana Pie

2 or 3 bananas (sliced in shell).
1 c. b. sugar (slightly caramelled).
1 tbsp. butter.

Beat in double boiler 2 egg
yolks. 1 tbsp. each flour
and cornstarch and mix
these five ingredients well
then add enough boiling
water to make paste
required thickness.
Cool slightly before pouring
over bananas in baked shell.

Mary G. Duff

Pineapple Pie

2 tbsp. cornstarch
½ c. sugar
½ tsp. salt
1 No. 2 can Libby's Crushed Pineapple
2 eggs (separated)
1 tbsp. lemon juice
Baked pastry shell

Mix first three ingredients. Add pineapple. Cook until clear and thickened. Add beaten yolks and cook 1 min. Cool. Add lemon juice. Pour into baked shell. Top with meringue made by folding 4 tbsp. sugar into stiffly beaten egg whites. Brown in 325° oven. Makes one eight inch pie.

Verna D. Smith
(Mrs. Russell G.)

202

Coconut Cream Pie

2 Cups Milk
3/4 " Sugar
1 " shredded Coconut
3 eggs
3 tblsp. flour
1/2 tsp. salt.

Heat milk and sugar to the boiling point. Mix flour with cold milk or water, add egg yolks and pour slowly into the boiling milk stirring constantly. Cook until thick. Add coconut and salt. Pour into a baked shell. Garnish with meringue made of the egg whites and 1/4 cup Sugar. Brown in a moderate oven.

Libbie M. Deal
(Mrs. J. W.)

Chocolate Bavarian Pie

1 tbsp. gelatine
¼ c. cold water
3 slightly beaten egg yolks
½ c. sugar
1 tsp. salt
1 c. scalded milk
1 tsp. vanilla
3 egg whites beaten stiff
½ c. heavy cream (whipped)

Soften gelatine in water. Combine egg-yolks, sugar, salt. Slowly add milk. Cook in double boiler until mixture coats spoon. Add softened gelatine. Stir until dissolved. Cool. Add vanilla. Fold in eggwhites and cream. Pour into crust. Sprinkle with ¼ c. chocolate wafer crumbs. Chill thoroughly.

Crumb Crust:
Blend 1¼ c. chocolate wafer crumbs with ⅛ c. melted butter. Press into pie dish. Chill.

Alice Adams
(Mrs. E. C.)

204

Delicious Butter Tarts

1 cup brown sugar
1 cup corn syrup
1 tsp vanilla
2 eggs
⅛ lb. butter

Cream butter add sugar, corn
syrup and vanilla. Stir eggs (do
not beat) in another bowl add
to mixture and stir. Put in baked
pastry shells in which raisins
(soaked in hot water) have been
dropped in bottoms. Nuts and
cocoanut may be put in if desired
Bake 15 min. in hot oven. Yield
1 doz. large.

Mona G. Rhodenizer
(Mrs H. A.)

Brown
Sugar

205

Paste for Tarts, Tartlets etc.

Ingredients : -

½ lb. flour

4 ozs. shortening or butter

1 yolk of egg

1 tsp. baking powder

1 tsp sugar

Pinch of salt.

About ⅓ pint of water.

Method :-

Rub. the shortening lightly into the flour, add the baking powder, salt, egg yolk, and as much water as is necessary to form a stiff paste. Roll out to the required thickness and use at once.

Rosa Friesen
(Mrs. P. K.)

206

Lemon Cheese

Ingredients :-
  Rind and juice of 2 lemons
  3 eggs
  2 ozs butter
  ½ lb sugar

Method :-
  Grate the rind of the lemons
and squeeze out the juice
Beat the eggs, add other
ingredients and cook in
double boiler until it becomes
thick.
  Good for tarts, jelly roll,
and cake filling.

Rosa Iversen
(Mrs. P.K.)

209

Cream Puffs.

1 cup hot water.
½ cup butter.
1 cup sifted flour.
3 eggs.

Boil butter and water together and while boiling stir in the flour. Take from the stove and beat to paste.

When this cools add the unbeaten eggs one at a time, beating after each egg is added. Stir five minutes and drop in tablespoonful on a buttered tin. Bake in quick oven twenty five minutes.

Cream for filling — 1 cup milk, ½ cup sugar, 1 egg, 3 tablespoonfuls flour. Flavor to taste. When puffs and cream are cold, open puffs with a knife and put in cream.

Elfreda. A. Masner
(Mrs Charles.)

208

Cheese Straws

1 cup grated cheese
1 cup pastry flour
1 tsp. Baking Powder
4 tbsps. milk
2 tbsps. butter
yolk of 1 egg
pinch of salt
pinch of cayenne pepper

Cut and rub butter in flour like pie paste. Then add cheese, salt & pepper, and baking powder. Mix with egg yolk and milk Roll out dough and cut in long narrow strips Bake in fairly hot oven.

Edythe E. Oxner
(Mrs. J. W.)

211

Strawberry Shortcake

2 cups sifted flour
4 tsp. B. P
½ tsp. salt
⅓ cup sugar
½ cup heavy cream
¼ cup water
½ cup shortening

Mix and sift flour, baking powder, salt and
sugar. Combine water and cream.
Cut in shortening until mixture looks
like coarse corn meal   Add cream
quickly, stirring until dough follows
spoon around the bowl. Drop by
spoonful on baking sheet.
Flatten a little and bake in hot
oven (450°) 10 minutes.
Split and butter while hot. Put sweetened
crushed berries between the biscuits. Cover with
whipped cream and garnish with whole
berries.

Muriel E. Hell.
(Mrs. E. H.)

Just Desserts

211

Ice Cream

"Basic Recipe for Ice Cream"
Frozen in an Ice Cream Freezer.

3 cups scalded Milk
1½ cups Sugar.
1 tsp Salt.
6 egg Yolks
1 qt heavy Cream.

Method. — Mix sugar, salt & egg Yolks. Pour on milk. Cook in double boiler until mixture coats spoon. Cool. Add cream & flavoring.

Nougat Ice Cream!

Add. — ⅓ c. each pistachio, filbert, English walnuts & almond meats. ½ c. Bacardi rum, ¼ c. caramelized sugar, 1 tsp extract almond, 1 tsp vanilla.

Have ready freezer, crushed ice and rock salt. Place can in Tub. Put in dasher and fill can only ⅔ full (To allow for expansion during freezing.)

Fill Tub with alternate layers of ice and salt. Crank steadily until frozen.

Mabel G. Zwicker.
(Mrs. H. F.)

212

WE'VE HAD
BAKED ALASKA
FOR DINNER!

Bake hot milk cake in rectangular pan. Cut cake in half making two layers. Only one layer is used.
Shortly before serving, beat 6 large egg whites with ½ tsp cream of tartar until stiff. Beat in gradually 1 cup sugar. Continue beating hard until meringue is stiff and glossy.
Place cooled cake on several thicknesses of wrapping paper on a wet board. Pile 1½ qt. ice cream on cake leaving a good half inch margin around cake. Completely cover ice cream and sides of cake with a thick coating of meringue.

     Temperature: 500° - very hot oven.
     Time: 3 to 5 min (just until meringue is delicately browned)
Slip dessert from board onto serving platter. Serve at once.

          Jean B. Morrow (Mrs. C.J)

Grape Sherbet

1 C grape juice
1 orange (juice only)
1 C milk and cream mixed
  or use top of quart bottle
¾ C sugar

Mix sugar and cream together,
add grape juice and orange
juice. Stir together and put in
an electric refrigerator to freeze
for three hours at highest degree
Stir every half hour to make
creamy. Serves 5 to 6 portions

Christabel Cantelope
(Mrs. D. C.)

214

Maple Mousse

1 cup boiled rice

Boil in 3 qts water and salt for ½ hr., drain, pour cold water over rice and drain again.

½ pt. whipping cream
1 egg white

Beat cream and egg white separately until stiff. Fold in with rice, put in mold and chill.

Sauce

1 cup maple syrup
2 egg yolks (beaten)

Boil together until it thickens. Beat other egg white stiff and mix into thickened mixture.

Peggy Rhuland.
(Mrs. F. A.)

SNOW PUDDING
--> --> -->

½ box gelatine
1 c. sugar
2 c. Boiling water
Juice of 2 lemons
het cool, then beat whites of 4 eggs stiff
Beat in with gelatine mixture until
it stands in peaks. For an added
attraction take ⅓ of pudding and add
a few drops of yellow colouring and
fold into mixture.

CUSTARD

4 Egg yolks, 1 pint of milk, ½ c. sugar,
pinch of salt. Cook in double boiler
and watch carefully until spoon is
coated with mixture. Add vanilla
when cool.

Myrtle Bellinger
(Mrs. Anson)

216

BLUE ROCKS
Favorite Haunt of Artists

BACKMAN

Prune Whip

3 Eggs
½ cup powdered Sugar
¾ lb. Prunes cooked and chopped

Whip egg whites stiff, add sugar beating constantly. Then add Prunes. Serve in sherbet glasses with custard.

Custard

Cook 3 egg yolks with 1 cup milk and 1 tbsp. sugar in a double boiler until mixture coats the spoon. Add Vanilla. Whipped cream may be added

Hazel Smith Geldert
(Mrs. E. C.)

218

Lemon Fluff

3 T. cornstarch	1½ c. hot milk
1 c. sugar	2 egg yolks
1 T. flour	½ c. lemon juice
¼ t. salt	Grated rind 2 lemons
½ c cold milk	2 egg whites

Mix dry ingredients with cold milk.
Add to hot milk in double boiler. Cook
until thickened & cornstarch taste
gone. Add egg yolks (beaten) & grated
rind Cook 5 minutes. Remove from
heat & add lemon juice Beat into
stiffly beaten egg whites

Anne Maycock (Mrs. N.T.)

219

Lemon Sponge Pudding

1 cup white sugar
1 tablespoon butter
2 heaping teaspoons flour
pinch of salt
1 lemon
2 eggs
1 cup milk

Cream together butter, sugar, flour, salt, lemon juice and rind of lemon. Add well beaten egg yolks, milk, and lastly well beaten egg whites. Pour filling in pudding dish and bake in moderate oven.

Elsie Heimmelman
(Mrs George)

220

Marshmallow Pudding

1 c. cherries
1 tbsp. cherry syrup
½ c. walnuts
½ lb. marshmallows
1 c. heavy cream
2 tbsp. pul. sugar
½ tsp. vanilla

Cut cherries into pieces and add syrup. Cut walnuts and marshmallows into 5 pieces. Whip cream, add sugar and vanilla and fold in remaining ingredients. Turn into a mould and let stand until firm. (2 hrs.) White grapes, strawberries or pineapple may be substituted.

Verna D. Smith
(Mrs. Russell J.)

Irish Moss Blanc Mange.

3/4 cup Irish Moss
1 quart water
1 16 oz. tin evaporated milk
   pinch salt.   1 teaspoon flavoring
Wash Irish Moss and soak for
thirty minutes. Using a double
boiler. To the Irish Moss add one
quart water. Boil until thick.
strain, add milk, salt and
flavoring Pour into molds to set.
Serve with sugar and cream.
Fruit may be added if desired.
you can obtain Irish Moss at low
tide off the Nova Scotia coast. It
grows on rocks and ledges.

Jennie E. Smeltzer.

(Mrs. E. S.)

Orange Pudding

Peel and cut five Oranges into slices and pour 1 cup sugar over them. Heat 1 pt milk to boiling point, add yolks 3 Eggs well beaten and 1 tbsp cornstarch made smooth in cold milk. Stir all the time and pour over fruit as soon as it thickens. Beat whites 3 Eggs stiff, add 1 tsp sugar and spread over top. Set in oven one minute to harden.

Leila E. D. Kinley

Pineapple Tapioca Pudding

1 pint milk
2 eggs
3 heaping tablespoons Minute Tapioca
¾ cup sugar
¼ tsp. salt

Put milk on stove to heat in a double boiler.

Beat eggs. Add sugar, tapioca and salt

Pour hot milk over last mixture.

Cook and stir until it becomes thick

Cool

Add one tin or less of crushed pineapple

Garnish with whipped cream.

(Mrs Ray) Norma R. Tanner.

Rice Pudding

½ cup (scant) dry rice
¾ cup sugar
qrt. milk
Nutmeg and salt to taste
Piece of butter size of a
small egg.   Mix
altogether and put in
buttered casserole.
Bake 1½ hr., stirring
often

Frances B. Sterne
(Mrs. R. C.)

Chocolate Fluff Pudding

2 z. chocolate
1¾ c. milk
1 c. bread cubes
1 tbsp. butter

3 eggs
¼ tsp. salt
¾ c. sugar
1 tsp. vanilla

Cut up chocolate and place in double boiler, add milk and heat until chocolate melts beat smooth and heat to scalding point. Add this to the bread cubes placed in greased baking dish with butter and salt. Beat egg yolks slightly and add sugar, add to milk mixture. Fold in stiffly beaten egg whites and vanilla. Sprinkle with chopped almonds. Place in pan of hot water and bake at 325° until set. Katherine B. Bourque (Mrs. D. J.)

Golden Pudding

1 cup of coconut	2 tablespoon lemon juice
3 " milk	2 teaspoon " rind
1½ crumbs.	2 eggs.
½ " sugar.	2 oranges.

Scald coconut in milk ½ hour. add crumbs and sugar. and cook in double boiler 15 minutes add lemon juice and rind to beaten egg yolks, and add to mixture — Pour into buttered baking dish — Place cut orange sprinkled with sugar on top. Cover with stiffly beaten egg white sweetened. Brown in moderate oven for 30 minutes and serve hot or cold. Serves 6.

(Mrs W.B.)

227

Nut Pudding with Ginger Sauce

1/4 cup butter
1/2 cup granulated sugar
1/2 cup milk
1/2 cup chopped walnuts
1 3/4 cups all-purpose flour
3 teaspoons baking powder
1/4 teaspoon salt
white of 1 egg

Mix the ingredients together reserving 1/2 cup flour in which to toss the nuts before adding to the mixture. Steam pudding in buttered mold 1 1/2 hours. Serve with ginger sauce.

Ginger Sauce

1 cup granulated sugar
1 cup water
yolk of 1 egg
1/4 teaspoon vanilla
2 tablespoons preserved ginger (minced)
or   ginger marmalade
1 tablespoon butter

Boil sugar and water for five minutes. Pour syrup slowly over beaten egg yolk, stirring constantly. Cook until mixture thickens a little, add butter vanilla and ginger. Serve hot.

Florence L. Eisenhauer.
(Mrs C.R.)

228

Honeycomb Pudding.

½ cup sugar
½ cup butter
1 cup milk
½ cup flour
4 eggs
1 tsp. soda
½ pint molasses

Beat together sugar, butter, milk and flour.

Add the eggs, well beaten

Into the molasses put 1 tsp. soda and stir until it foams, then add to the mixture

Steam in mould for one and a half hours.

Serve with hard sauce

Phoebe V. Conrad
229   (Mrs R. D.)

Hurry-up Pudding

1 cup flour
1 cup sugar
2 tsp. B. Powder
$\frac{1}{2}$ cup milk
1 cup raisins or dates

Sift together dry ingredients
add milk and mix well.
Then add raisins or dates
Bake in a moderate oven,
and serve with whipped cream.

Florence E. Hewat
(Mrs. W. A.)

PRIZE GINGER BREAD

½ c. sugar
½ c. butter and shortening mixed
1 Egg
1 c. molasses
2½ c. flour sifted
1½ tsp. soda
1 tsp. ginger
1 tsp. cinnamon
½ tsp. salt
½ tsp. cloves
1 c. hot water

Cream shortening and butter and sugar.
Add beaten egg; molasses; then dry
ingredients which have been sifted together.
Add hot water last and beat until smooth.
This batter is soft but makes a fine
cake. Bake in a greased pan 8 x 8, 35
minutes in a moderate oven or until
done.

Myrtle Ballinger
(Mrs. Anson)

231

Pineapple Upside Down Cake

3 Eggs
1 c. sugar
1½ c. pastry flour
1⅓ tsp. baking powder
½ c. water
1 tsp. vanilla

Cover pan with brown sugar, dot with butter. Put slices of pineapple on top. Bake at 350° for one hour.

Dorothy E. Geldert
(Mrs. L. W.)

TRIFLE

Any desired plain sponge layers cut in strips and spread generously with jam (strawberry or raspberry) or jelly (currant or grape). Place one-quarter of cake and jam strips criss cross in bowl and cover completely with chilled custard sauce (recipe below). Repeat until cake and custard are used, ending with custard. Chill overnight, or at least 8 hours. Top with whipped cream and sprinkle with finely chopped nuts.

CUSTARD SAUCE

6 tbsp flour
1 cup sugar
⅛ tsp. salt

4 eggs
4 cups milk
2 tsp. vanilla extract

Mix flour, sugar and salt. Beat eggs slightly; add. Scald milk; gradually add. Cook over hot water, stirring constantly, until mixture thickens and coats spoon. Cool. Add vanilla. Chill. Makes 4 cups.

Brandy, sherry or rum to taste may replace vanilla.

Edwena L. Anderson
(Mrs. K. B.)

233

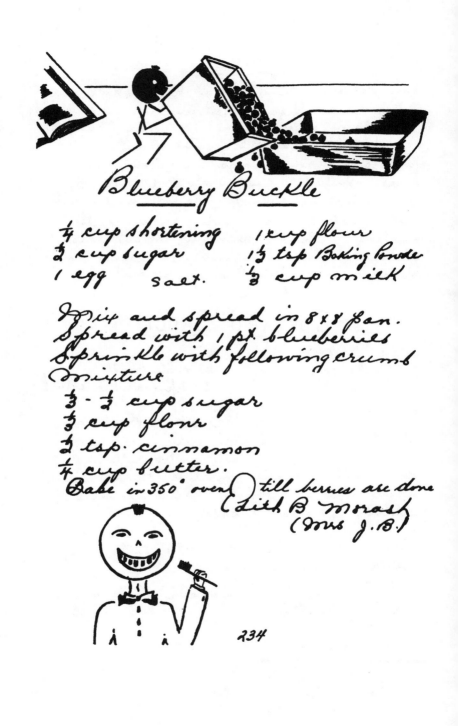

Blueberry Buckle

¼ cup shortening 1 cup flour
½ cup sugar 1½ tsp Baking Powder
1 egg salt. ⅓ cup milk

Mix and spread in 8 x 8 pan.
Spread with 1 pt blueberries
Sprinkle with following crumb
mixture

⅓ - ½ cup sugar
⅓ cup flour
½ tsp. cinnamon
¼ cup butter.
Bake in 350° oven till berries are done

Lith B Morash
(Mrs J. B.)

Apple Spice Pudding

1½ cups (full) grated apple
½ cup raisins,
½ cup (cut) dates
a few cherries (cut in halves)
1 cup sifted bread flour
¾ tsp soda, ½ tsp. salt.
½ tsp cinnamon, ¼ tsp nutmeg
½ c. shortening (or butter)
¾ c. white sugar, 1 egg
     1 Tbsp. cream.

Sift flour, soda, salt and spices.
Cream shortening, add sugar, cream well
Add beaten egg, then dry ingredients
and mix until blended. Add fruit,
apple and cream, folding in lightly.
Bake in pyrex baking dish in moderate
oven, 350° for 40 to 45 min.
   Serve hot with hard sauce or
any favorite pudding sauce.

                    Georgie M. Mason (Mrs H.F.)
                       235

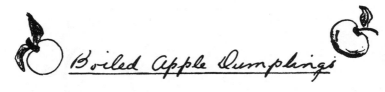

Boiled Apple Dumplings

½ dozen cooking apples, peeled
and cored. Make a biscuit
dough and roll about a half
an inch thick. Cut in rounds
and fold around apples.
Boil slowly twenty minutes.
Take out and break open,
spread with butter and
sprinkle with brown sugar.
Serve with or without cream.

Caramel Bread Pudding

¾ cup brown sugar   1½ cup milk
1 egg, beaten   1 tsp. vanilla
2 slices heavily buttered bread.
    Pack sugar in a buttered
casserole, cut bread in small pieces
and place buttered side down
on sugar. Mix egg, milk and
vanilla and pour over mixture.
Put in oven and bake until nicely
browned. Serve with or without
cream.

Emily Smith
236 (Mrs J. N.)

Caramel Dumplings

1 c. brown sugar   2 tbsps. butter
    1½ c. water

Caramelige sugar and butter.
Add water and boil a few minutes.

Batter –
  ½ c. white sugar   1 c. sifted flour
  2 tbsps. butter   1 tsp. B. P.
  ½ c. milk   salt
    Drop in syrup and bake in
oven 400° F. for 20 min. or until done.

Agnes P. Sweeny
(Mrs. D. L.)

Ironbound Steamed Pudding.

½ cup shortening   1 tsp. soda
½ cup white sugar   ¾ cup. buttermilk
1 egg.   ½ tsp. cinnamon
½ cup molasses   ¼ tsp. pastry spice
2 tbsp. thick cream   dash of nutmeg
1 tsp. salt.   3 cups flour (or
1 tsp. baking powder   enough to stiffen)

Combine in order given, turn into
a steamer and steam 2 hours (or
more (until done).

Sauce.

1 cup brown sugar   2 cups boiling water
3 tbsp. flour   2 tbsp. butter.
¼ tsp. salt.

Combine sugar, flour and salt in
saucepan. Add boiling water gradually,
stirring constantly. Cook over low heat,
stirring constantly, until thick and
smooth (about 5 minutes). Remove from
heat, add butter. Serve warm.

Mrs. Percy A. Young.

Steamed Chocolate Pudding

1 square chocolate
butter size of an egg
4 tbsp sugar
1 egg
1 cup flour
1 tsp. B powder
½ cup milk

Melt chocolate and butter. Add sugar and beaten egg. Add dry ingredients alternately with milk.

Sauce

Cream ½ cup butter and 1 cup brown sugar. Thicken 1½ cups water with 1½ tsp. corn starch or flour and add a little salt. Then pour over butter and sugar beating vigorously. The sauce will be foamy.

Josephine Eisenhauer
(Mrs. D. A.)

239

Steamed Blueberry Pudding.

1/4 C. shortening
2/3 C. sugar
1 well beaten egg
1 1/2 C. blueberries

1 C. milk
2 1/4 C. flour
4 tsps B.P.
vanilla

salt

Steam one hour.

Flora Dora Sauce

white of 1 egg
3/4 C. pulverized sugar
vanilla
yolk of 1 egg
3/4 C. heavy cream
salt

Beat egg white stiff. Add sugar
while beating. Add egg yolk beaten
then cream beaten stiff.

Jas. D. Lohnes
(Mrs. G. Ray)

STEAMED DATE PUDDING

½ cup Butter
1 cup Sugar
2 eggs
½ cup Bran
½ cup Milk
2 tsp. Baking Powder
½ tsp. Salt
1½ cups Flour
10 oz. Chopped Dates

Cream Butter and add sugar gradually, Then beaten eggs and other ingredients alternately with milk.
Steam for 2 hours.
Serve with Creamy Sauce or Lemon Sauce

CREAMY SAUCE

Beat 1 egg and 2 egg yolks until thick and creamy.
Beat in ½ cup sugar and ¼ tsp. Salt gradually and thoroly.
When thick, fold in ½ cup Whipped Cream

Gladys B. Smith

241

Plum Pudding

1½ cups suet
3 cups stale bread crumbs.
1½ cups grated carrot
6 egg yolks
1¼ cups brown sugar
1 cup molasses
Grated rind 2 lemons
½ cup brandy (or grape juice)
1¼ cups flour

Chop finely
2 cups seeded raisins
1 cup currants
2 oz. candied orange peel
2 oz. citron
2 tsp salt
1 tsp cinnamon
1 tsp. grated nutmeg
½ tsp. cloves

6 egg whites

Put suet through food chopper. Add bread crumbs and carrot. Beat egg yolks, add sugar gradually. Combine mixtures, add molasses, lemon rind and brandy. Add chopped fruits dredged with sifted flour, salt and spices to mixture. Lastly fold in stiffly beaten egg whites. Turn into buttered mold, garnished with cherries & almonds. Steam 5 hours.

Hard Sauce

Cream ⅓ cup butter ; add gradually 1 cup brown sugar, and 2 Tbsp. brandy (or vanilla) drop by drop

Joyce L. Tupper
(Mrs. J. A.)

242

Lemon Sauce

½ cup sugar
2 tbsp. butter
1 tbsp. cornstarch

1 tbsp. grated lemon rind
2 tbsp. lemon juice
1 cup water
salt

Mix cornstarch, sugar, lemon rind and salt. Gradually add water and lemon juice. Cook over low heat, stirring constantly, until thickened, then continue cooking 5 minutes. Remove from heat and add butter.

Fluff Sauce

2 tbsp. cornstarch
¼ cup sugar
¼ tsp. salt
2 cup milk

3 egg yolks
3 egg whites
few grains nutmeg
1 tbsp. either orange juice, pineapple juice, or sherry flavoring.

Combine cornstarch, sugar, salt, gradually add milk. Cook over hot water, stirring constantly, until thickened. Beat egg yolks, slowly add milk mixture. Cook over hot water, stirring, until mixture thickens and coats spoon. Beat egg whites stiff, fold in milk mixture. Cool, add flavoring and nutmeg. Serve with hot fruit puddings.

Edith B. Morash
(Mrs. J. B.)

243

Chocolate Sauce

2 squares chocolate   ½ cup sugar
¾ cup water   1 tsp. vanilla extract
    Salt

Combine chocolate and water and boil until thick, stirring constantly. Add sugar, salt, stir until dissolved. Bring to a boil and boil 2 minutes. Remove from heat, add vanilla.

Chocolate Milk Syrup.

Mix 2 tbsp of above chocolate sauce to each cup cold milk.

Butterscotch Sauce.

1 cup brown sugar   2 tbsp. corn syrup
½ cup granulated sugar   1 cup heavy cream

Mix together brown and white sugar and corn syrup. Cook to medium-firm ball stage. Remove from fire, let stand until almost cold, then stir in cup of heavy cream

Edith B. Morash
(Mrs. J. B.)

244

CAKE

245

Old Scripture Cake

1 cup Judges 5:25
2 cups Jeremiah 6:20
3½ " 1st Kings 4:22
3 " Samuel 30:12
1 cup Genesis 43:11
1 " Exodus 3:8
5 Isiah 10:14
A little Leviticus 2:13
A few kinds of 1st Kings 10:2
1 large spoon Genesis 24:20
Follow Solomons advice
for making a good boy
(Proverbs 23:14) and you
will have a good cake.

Ida E Himmelman

(Mrs L.A.H.)

Daffodil Cake

Yolks of 6 eggs well beaten with $\frac{1}{2}$ cup of sugar and 2 tablespoonfuls of water for 15 minutes. Add $\frac{1}{2}$ cup of flour and 1 teaspoon of baking powder.

White part.

Whites of 6 eggs beaten until stiff, Add $\frac{1}{2}$ cup of sugar, $\frac{1}{4}$ tsp. of salt, $\frac{1}{2}$ cup of flour and $\frac{1}{2}$ tsp. cream of tartar.

Put white in bottom of pan and spread yellow over it. Use lemon flavouring for white mixture and vanilla for yellow. Bake one hour

E. Anderson
(Mrs. Roseville)

247

Hot Milk Cake

3 Eggs
1½ c. Sugar
2 tsp. butter
3/4 c. milk
2 tsp. lemon Extract
1½ c. flour (Swans Down)
2 tsp. baking powder.

Sift together 3 times flour, baking powder and salt. Beat Eggs until light and foamy. Gradually add Sugar. Add flavoring. Fold in flour mixture. Combine milk and butter; heat. Quickly add to egg flour mixture. Stir until smooth. Bake in 9" tube pan. in 350°F oven.

Jean C. Rofuse
(Mrs. E. W.)

JELLY ROLL

$\frac{3}{4}$ c. flour
$\frac{3}{4}$ tsp. baking powder
4 eggs
$\frac{3}{4}$ c. sugar
1 tsp. vanilla
$\frac{1}{4}$ tsp. salt
        Jelly

Combine baking powder, salt, eggs in bowl. Place over smaller bowl of hot H_2O, and beat with beater. Add sugar gradually. Remove bowl from H_2O, add flour & vanilla.

Bake 400° — 13 minutes, on greased wax paper in oblong pan. Turn out on wax paper sprinkled with sugar. Spread with jelly and roll.

Dorothy E. Geldert
(Mrs. L. W.)

Cream Pie Cake

3 eggs (well beaten)

1 C sugar (scant)

1 C flour (swansdown)

2 T cold water

1 tsp. baking powder

1 pinch salt

vanilla

Beat eggs well, add sugar gradually; beating well after each addition. Fold in flour to which baking powder and salt have been added. Stir in cold water and bake in tube pan or two pie tins.

Cream Filling

1 C milk scalded, 1 egg in dish, 3 T sugar, 3 level T flour, pinch salt. Mix ingredients with spoon and stir in hot milk. Cook in double boiler.

Christabel Cantelope
250   (mrs. D. C.)

Never Fail Chocolate Cake

2 Tbsp. Butter
2 Squares Chocolate
1 Cup Sugar
1 Egg
1½ cups Flour
1 tsp. Baking Soda
Pinch Salt
1 cup Sour Milk
1 tsp. Vanilla

Melt butter and chocolate over hot water. Mix with sugar. Add well beaten egg. Sift together flour, salt and soda and add to first mixture, alternately with the sour milk. Add vanilla and beat well. Pour into greased pan (8" square) and bake for 40 minutes in moderate oven (350°).

If heavy sour cream is used instead of milk, butter may be omitted

Gladys B. Smith

251

Chocolate Cake

2½ squares of chocolate.
2 tbsp white sugar.
5 tbsp water.
cook till thick, leave cool.

cream: ½ cup butter.
1½ cups brown sugar.
2 eggs. add chocolate mixture

Sit quite 2½ cups sifted cake flour.
1 tsp soda.
1 tsp cream of tartar.
Add 1 cup milk alternately
with flour mixture.
dash of salt.
1 tsp vanilla.
Bake 1 hour at 350°.

Freda M. Smith.
(Mrs R. G.)

252

Spice Cake

1 scant cup butter
1 cup sugar
3 eggs (2 whites may be saved for frosting)
1 cup boiling water
1½ cups flour
1 tsp. soda
1 tsp. cinnamon, allspice, cloves or
        any spices.
1 cup raisins
1 cup chopped nuts.

Put raisins in a bowl, sprinkle soda over them, then pour over them the boiling water. Let stand until cool. Mix butter and sugar, add eggs, flour, spices, raisins and water. This cake looks thin, do not add more flour.

Honey Icing

Boil 1 cup of honey until it spins a good double thread when dropped from a spoon. Pour over two egg whites beaten stiff. Keep beating until frosting holds shape

Frances B. Sterne
(Mrs. R. C.)

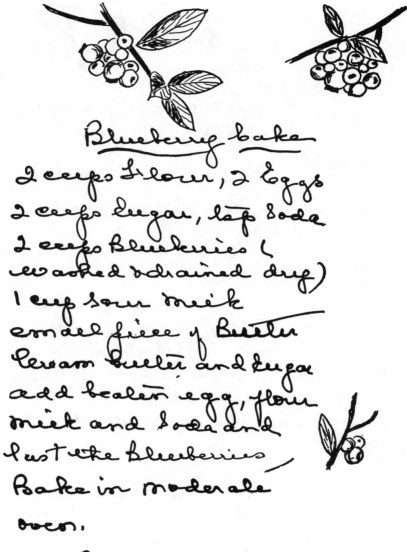

Blueberry bake

2 cups Flour, 2 Eggs
2 cups Sugar, tsp Soda
2 cups Blueberries (
washed & drained dry)
1 cup sour milk
small piece of Butter
Cream butter and sugar
add beaten egg, flour
milk and soda and
last the Blueberries
Bake in moderate
oven.

Leila E.D. Kinley.
(Mrs J.J.)

Queen Elizabeth Cake.

¼ cup butter
1 cup white sugar
1 egg well beaten
1½ cups sifted flour
¼ tsp. salt
1 tsp. Baking Powder
1 tsp. soda
½ cup chopped nuts
1 cup boiling water over
1 cup chopped dates
1 tsp. vanilla

Cream butter and sugar, add egg and the remaining ingredients in order. Bake in angel cake pan for 45 minutes at 375°

Icing

5 large tbsps. brown sugar
½ cup coconut
3 tbsps. butter
2 tbsps. cream
Boil 3 minutes and pour over cake while warm.

Bessie S. Iversen
(Mrs. L.J.)

Chocolate Marble Cake

3 cups sifted cake flour
3 tsps. Baking Powder
⅓ " salt
¾ cup butter
2¼ cups sugar
¾ cup milk
1 tsp. vanilla
6 egg whites, stiffly beaten
3 squares Baker's unsweetened chocolate, melted
4 tbsps. sugar
¼ c. boiling water
¼ tsp. soda

Melt chocolate over hot water and add next three ingredients in order given. Cool.

Sift flour once, measure and sift again with B.P. + salt. Cream butter thoroughly, add sugar gradually and cream until fluffy. Add flour mixture alternately with milk, beating after each addition until smooth. Add vanilla. Fold in egg whites quickly + thoroughly. Divide batter in two parts, adding chocolate mixture to one part, blending well. Put by tablespoons into a greased 10 x 7 x 3 pan alternately dark + light mixture. Bake in a 350° or 375° oven about 55 minutes.

Icing

2 squares Baker's chocolate, melted
1½ cups icing sugar   2 tbsps. hot water
3 egg yolks   4 tbsps butter

To melted chocolate add sugar and hot water. Blend well. Add egg yolks, one at a time. Beat well. Add butter + beat well. Cut up marshmallows maybe added.

Evelyn V. Zinck
(Mrs. B. E.)

256

JACK and JERRY CAKE

1 Cup butter
2 Cups Sugar
3 Eggs
1 Cup Milk

3 cups Flour { 1½ c Swansdown
                1½ c Pastry

1 Tsp. Baking Powder
Salt — Vanilla
Divide batter into 2 parts
  To one part add
1 tsp Cloves — 1 tsp Cinnamon
¼ cup Raisins — ¼ cup Walnuts
2 Tbsp. Molasses
Place this part (dark) on bottom of pan
Place other part on top
Bake at 350°

Audrey M. Smith
Mrs. W.W.

Boiled Raisin Cake.

1 cup raisins } Boil until 1 cup
2 cups water } juice remains.
1 cup sugar
½ cup butter
1 egg (beaten)
¼ tsp salt
1 tsp ground cloves
1 tsp soda
vanilla.
2 cups flour

Cool juice, add soda. Cream butter
and sugar, add beaten egg. Mix dry
ingredients and raisin juice alternately. add raisins. Cook at 350°F
for 45 minutes in a small pan.

Peggy Rhuland.
(Mrs. F. A.)

258

Sponge Cake

5 large or 6 small eggs.
1½ cups white sugar
1½ cups flour.
⅓ teaspoon cream tartar,
a pinch of salt, and flavor to taste

Method.

Measure, sift and set aside flour.
Separate the eggs, beating the whites
into a stiff froth, adding sugar
slowly, also cream of tartar, and
salt last. Beat the yolks together
and add whites. Lastly add flour
slowly, add lemon or almond flavoring.
Bake in a tube pan in a moderate
oven from 35 to 45 minutes. Cool
cake before removing from pan.

Mary C. Oxner
(Mrs. S. W.)

259

Birthday Cake

1 cup. butter
2 " Sugar
3 eggs.
3½ cups. flour.
1/3 " Milk.
1 tsp. B.P.
(Use cake flour)   1 " lemon.

Method: Cream butter and Sugar.
Add whole eggs, one at a time,
beating five minutes after each
addition — Add flour, B.P. and salt
alternately with milk. Flavor
with lemon. Bake 1½ hours in
moderate oven.

Hilda M. Young
(Mrs. D. E.)

Almost As Good As Pound Cake

1 cup butter
1 cup sugar
3 eggs separated
2 cups flour (sifted)
½ cup milk
1 tsp. baking powder
1 tsp. vanilla
1 tsp. lemon

By adding cherries, sultana raisins and candied pineapple - makes an excellent white fruit cake. If adding fruit, measure the 2 cups of flour before sifting it and add whites of eggs last (fold in)

Method:

Cream sugar and butter together until all sugar granules are dissolved. Add unbeaten egg yolks and beat thoroughly. Sift flour, add baking powder and sift again. Add flour and milk alternately to mixture and mix carefully. Add flavouring, and egg whites Bake 350° for 60 minutes.

B. Jean Morrow
(Mrs. C. J.).

261

Pound Cake

1 lb. Sugar
1 lb. Butter
1 lb. Eggs (8 large)
1 lb. (scant) all-purpose
    Flour (3¾ cups)
½ tsp. Baking Powder
1 tsp. Salt
½ tsp. Lemon Rind
2 Tbsp. Lemon Juice
½ tsp. Lemon Extract

Cream butter, add sugar slowly
and cream well.
Add flavoring and beaten egg yolks.
Sift together flour, baking powder and
salt, and add.
Beat only until smooth, then fold in
the beaten egg whites.
Bake in a loaf pan, which has been
lined with 3 layers of brown paper –
Butter top layer.
Tie a piece of brown paper over the
cake and bake in a slow oven –
300° for 2 hrs. Remove top paper and
bake another half hour (if necessary)

Antoinette E. Smith
(Mrs. B.C.)

262

St. John's - Lunenburg
Anglican
THE SECOND OLDEST PROTESTANT CHURCH
IN BRITISH NORTH AMERICA

White Fruit Cake

1 lb. butter — 1 lb. granulated sugar — 8 eggs,
1 lb. flour — 1 tsp. baking powder — 1 tsp. salt,
¼ cup brandy — 1 lb. white sultana raisins.
¾ lb. candied red and green pineapple — ½ lb. citron.
1 lb. blanched almonds — 1 large bottle maraschino cherries

Cream butter and sugar until fluffy. Beat 8 eggs
4 - at a time until thick. Add to first mixture,
then add flour, (reserving enough to dredge fruit)
mixed and sifted three times with baking powder and
salt, fruit (omitting cherries) ½ lb. blanched almonds,
(saving ½ lb. for top of cake)
chopped fine, then brandy.
Beat well and put half of batter
in pan. Arrange cherries (dipped
in extra flour) in rows. Cover with remainder
of batter and place split almonds upright on
top of cake. Bake in oven 300°F. for 1 hour,
then 325°F. for 2 hours.

Joyce L. Lupper (Mrs. J. A.)

264

Dark Fruit Cake

10 ozs. butter   5 eggs
1/2 lb. flour   1/2 lb dark brown sugar
1/2 cup molasses   1/2 cup strawberry preserves
1/2 cup brandy   1 tsp vanilla, drop or two
of bitter almond and rose extracts.
1 tsp. mace   1 1/2 nutmegs (grated)
1 Tbsp. clove   1 Tbsp. cinnamon
1 Tbsp. allspice   1/2 tsp. soda
1 pt. currants   3 pts. seeded raisins
1/4 lb. almonds blanched and cut up.
1/4 lb. of orange or lemon peel cut up
     1/2 lb. citron peel cut up.
2 Tbsps. flour mixed with fruit.

Cream butter and sugar, add eggs
one at a time unbeaten, molasses,
preserves, brandy and flavorings.
Then the spices and soda dissolved
   a little warm water. Next the flour
and the fruit last.
Steam steadily for 4 or 5 hours and
bake 1 hour in a slow oven. Allow
to cool in pan.

       Marion W. Zwicker
       (Mrs. F. Homer)

Icings

Quick Chocolate Frosting

1 cup sifted icing sugar
1 small egg
2 tbsp butter (softened)
½ tsp vanilla
⅛ c. milk
2 sq. unsweetened chocolate (melted)

Combine in order given, place bowl in a pan of ice cold water and beat with egg beater until stiff enough to put on cake.

Boiled Icing

1 egg white
¾ c. brown sugar
1 tsp corn syrup
2 tbsp cold water
½ tsp B. P.
1 tsp vanilla

Put all in double boiler on stove, and beat with egg beater seven minutes or until thick enough to spread on cake. Remove from heat, beat in B. P. and vanilla.

Mona Rhodeniger
(Mrs H. H.)

266

Butter Icing

4 tablespoons butter
few grains salt
2 cups sifted icing sugar
½ teaspoon vanilla
2 tablespoons (about) milk

Cream butter until soft; add salt
Work sugar into butter alternately
with milk to make a spreading consistency.
beat in vanilla. Spread on cold cake.
To make coffee butter icing substitute 2
tablespoons strong coffee for the milk
called for in above recipe.

Orange Butter Icing

1½ tsp grated orange rind
1 tablespoon orange juice
¼ tsp lemon juice
4 tablespoons butter
1 egg yolk
2 c. icing sugar

few grains salt and ¼ tsp vanilla
Combine orange rind and fruit juices
Cream butter, beat in egg yolk and salt
Work sugar into creamed mixture alternately
into juices — use just enough liquid to make
a frosting of spreading consistency; beat in
vanilla. Spread on cold cake.

Mona Rhodenizer
(Mrs H. H.)

269

Almond Paste

1 lb. almonds blanched
whites 2 eggs.
1 lb. icing sugar maybe little more.
2 tbsp almond extract
little rose water if desired
Put almonds thru food chopper.
Beat egg whites. Add almonds, sugar and
extract.

Peanut Butter Icing.

2 tablespoons butter
2 tablespoons peanut butter
few grains salt
1 1/4 c. sifted icing sugar
2 tsp lemon juice
1 tablespoon orange juice
few drops vanilla

Cream butter and peanut butter until
soft; add salt.
Work sugar into creamed mixture
alternately with fruit juices to make a
frosting of spreading consistency; beat in
vanilla. Spread on cold cake

Mona Rhodenizer
(Mrs A. H.

268

Cookies

269

The Misses Duffs Scotch Cakes

1 lb flour
½ lb butter
¼ lb brown sugar
mix well by hand roll out not too thin
bake in 350° oven about 15 minutes

Hermits

1 cup butter
1½ cups brown sugar
3 eggs well beaten
½ tsp soda dissolved in
2 tbsp hot water
½ cup chopped dates, ½ cup nuts
2 tsp baking powder, ½ tsp salt
¼ tsp. allspice, nutmeg, 1 tsp cinnamon
3 cups flour
mix in order given, sift dry ingredients
together and add gradually. Drop by
spoonfulls on a greased baking sheet.
Bake in 375° oven for about 15 minutes

Jean Burns Smith
(Mrs. Malcolm)

270

Sunny-day Cookies

Temp. 425°F   Time: 10-12 mins

1 cup butter
2 cups brown sugar
3 eggs - 2 tsp. vanilla
4½-15 cups flour
½ teaspoon salt
1 teaspoon soda
2 teaspoons cream of tartar

Cream together butter, sugar and vanilla. Add unbeaten eggs, one at a time, beating well after each addition. Add 4½ cups flour sifted with the remaining ingredients. If mixture is too soft add extra ½ cup flour.

Roll portions on floured board to ⅛th inch thickness, cut and bake as specified above on oiled cooky sheet.

Store in covered tin box when cool. Yield about 9 dozen.

Josephine Kaulbach
(Mrs. R. C. S.)

271

½ cup Butter
1 cup Sugar
1 egg (well beaten)
1¾ cups Flour
2 tsps. Baking Powder
½ tsp. Salt
1 tsp. Grated Orange or Lemon Rind

Cream the butter, add sugar
gradually; then well beaten egg.
Add flavoring and dry ingredients. Chill.
Toss on floured board, and roll ⅛ inch thick.
Cut with doughnut cutter, or in long narrow
strips.
Brush with egg white diluted with 2 Tbsp water
Sprinkle with 1 Tbsp. Sugar mixed with
¼ tsp. Cinnamon.
Decorate with blanched Almonds, Raisins or
Cherries.
Place on buttered sheet.
Bake in moderate oven 8 - 10 minutes.

Gladys B. Smith

— Butter Fingers —

$\frac{7}{8}$ c. shortening (mostly butter)
5 tbsp. sugar   1 tbsp. water
1 tsp. vanilla   1 c. chopped walnuts.
          2 c. flour

Cream shortening and sugar.
Add vanilla. Add flour
gradually, then add water
and nuts. Shape into oblong
cookies about the size of
a finger. Bake in 350° oven,
15-20 min. When cool, roll in
granulated sugar. Makes
about 3 dozen cookies.

— Oatmeal Cookies —

2½ c. rolled oats   2 eggs
2¼ c. flour   2 tbsp. milk
1 c. butter + shortening   1 tsp. soda
1 c. sugar   1 tsp. cinnamon

Roll thin and bake in hot
oven. Put two cookies together
with date filling.
Filling —
  1 lb. dates   Ettie Hamm.
  1 c. sugar   (Mrs. J. H.)
  1 c. water

273

Ginger Snaps

1 Cup Sugar
1 cup Molasses
1 cup Butter or shortening

1 Beaten Egg
1 Tbsp. Ginger
1 tsp. Cinnamon
1 tsp. Salt
1 Tbsp. Soda dissolved
in 1 Tbsp. Vinegar
Flour to roll.

Boil first three ingredients for 2 minutes When cool, add other ingredients, then flour enough to roll. Chill. Roll thin and bake on greased sheet in quick oven (450°) If preferred Ginger Snaps may be made like refrigerator cookies and sliced thinly. Gladys B. Smith

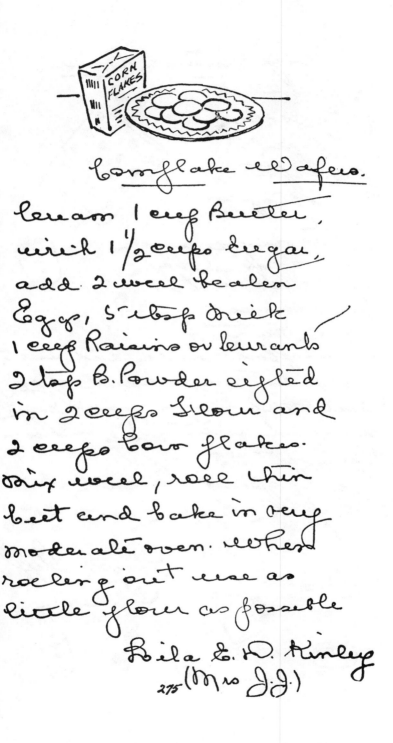

Cornflake Wafers.

Cream 1 cup Butter,
with 1½ cups Sugar,
add 2 well beaten
Eggs, 5 tbsp Milk
1 cup Raisins or currants
2 tsp B. Powder sifted
in 2 cups Flour and
2 cups corn flakes.
Mix well, roll thin
beat and bake in very
moderate oven. When
rolling out use as
little flour as possible

Leila E. D. Kinley
275 (Mrs J.J.)

Orange Oatmeal Rounds

1 c. flour
1/2 tsp. soda
1/2 tsp. salt
1 c. butter
2 1/c. b. sugar
1 egg
2 tbsp. orange juice
1 " orange rind
1 c. rolled oats
1/2 c. raisins
1/4 c. nuts

Sift flour, soda and salt.
Mix butter, sugar and egg.
Beat well. Stir in orange,
oats and nuts. Lastly flour.
Bake at 350°.
Drop by spoonfuls and pat
with fork dipped in milk.

Mary G. Duff

Oatmeal Squares

½ cup butter
1 cup brown sugar
2¼ cups Quick Robin Hood Oats
pinch of salt   1 tsp. vanilla

Melt butter, add sugar, oats,
salt, vanilla and mix well
together. Pat into pan, bake in
a moderate oven and cut when cool.

Florence E. Hewat

Delicious Drop Cookies

½ cup butter (or margarine)
1 cup brown sugar
½ tsp. soda, ½ tsp. cream of tartar
2 eggs
1¾ cups flour
1 heaping cup chopped dates and nuts
1 tsp. vanilla

Cream butter, sugar, then drop in
eggs, beat well. Add dry ingredients
and mix well, then fruit and vanilla.
Drop on greased cookie sheet, temp, 350°.

Florence E. Hewat
(Mrs. W. A.)

277

Chocolate Dot Cookies.

Cream 1c butter Add 3/4 c.
brown sugar, 3/4 c. white sugar.
2 eggs Dissolve 1 tsp soda in
1 tsp. hot water Add 2 1/4 c flour.
salt, vanilla Lastly 1 c chopped
nuts and 1 bar semi sweet
chocolate Drop by tsp. on
greased cookie sheet Bake
10 to 12 minutes in 375° oven.

Jean D Lohnes
(Mrs G Ray)

PURE
CANE
SUGAR

278

Frying pan Cookies

Drop following in cold
frying pan:
   2 unbeaten eggs
   1 c. sugar
   1½ c. dates (cut)
   salt

   Cook over a low heat
for 10 min. stirring
constantly. Remove from
stove and add 2 cups of
rice crispies.
   Roll in balls and dip
in cocoanut.

Mildred L. Rundle
(Mrs A. C.)

279

Ragged Robins

Whites of 2 eggs
1 cup white sugar
1 tsp vanilla
1 cup chopped nuts (walnuts)
1 cup chopped dates
¼ tsp. salt
2 cups crushed cornflakes.

Beat egg whites until light
add gradually the sugar
and salt — flavoring.
Lastly fold in nuts, dates
and cornflakes
Drop by teaspoonful on
buttered pan and bake
about a half hour. Temp 325

Hilda M. Robart
(Mrs V. D)

280

Christmas Cookies.

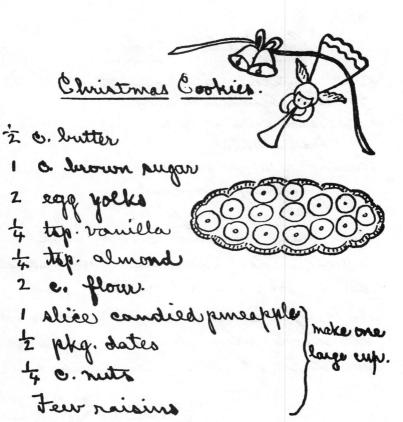

½ c. butter
1 c. brown sugar
2 egg yolks
¼ tsp. vanilla
¼ tsp. almond
2 c. flour.
1 slice candied pineapple ⎫ make one
½ pkg. dates   ⎬ large cup.
¼ c. nuts   ⎭
  Few raisins

Drop in pan,—place candied red cherry on top of each. Bake 15–20 m. in 375° oven.

Alice Adams.
(Mrs. E. C.)

281

"Cornflake Chews"

Boil together two minutes:
¾ cup brown sugar
3 ½ tbsps. corn syrup
1 tbsp. butter

Add: ½ cup dates
½ cup cocoanut
2 ½ cups cornflakes

Mix date mixture with boiled syrup, shape in macaroons and place on waxed paper. Put dab of peanut butter on top of each, then half a cherry on top of the peanut butter.

Bessie S. Sorensen
(Mrs. L.J.)

Almond Cookies

2 Egg whites
1 c. Pulverized sugar

Take 4 tsp. of the mixture and keep to drop on top of cookies,

To Remainder add
$\frac{1}{2}$ lb. Almond Nuts -ground-

Bake in a moderate oven for 30 minutes.

Mildred Adams Rilcey
(Mrs. E.E.)   283

Delights

1 cup brown sugar
2 eggs beaten
5 tsp. flour
1/2 tsp. Baking Powder
salt
1 tsp. vanilla

1 cup chopped dates
1 cup chopped nuts
1/2 cup cocoanut.
Sprinkle 4 tsp. flour
extra over last three
items and add last.

Bake in small cup
cake pans at 350°.

Audrey M. Smith
(Mrs. W. W.)

今 菜 大 樂 匯 代 燕

Unusual Chinese Chews

Beat well --- 2 eggs
Add ------ -- 1 cup sugar
Add ------ -- 3 tablespoons
                melted butter

Combine, add - 2 cups cut dates
              1/4 cup cut cherries
              1 tablespoon finely
              cut preserved ginger
Sift, measure - 3/4 cup flour
Re sift with - 1 teaspoon baking
                powder
              1/2 teaspoon salt

Add to first Mixture and combine
Turn into greased pan 9X12 and
bake in Mod. oven (350°F) 30 min.
When baked place cut marshmallows
on top, cover with any chocolate Icing
                Maud Morrow Bailly
              285 (Mrs. E.D.)

Marble Fudge Squares.

2 eggs
1 cup of brown sugar
1/4 cup of white sugar
1/2 tsp. salt
1 tsp. vanilla.

3/4 cup pastry flour
1 square melted chocolate
1 tbsp. butter
1/2 cup of chopped nuts

Beat eggs until light. Beat in brown sugar then white. Add flour, salt and vanilla. Mix well. Add nuts. Spread one-half of the mixture in an 8" pan. Add chocolate and butter melted together to remaining half and spread over top of the first mixture. Bake 20-25 minutes in an oven at 325 deg. F. Ice with a chocolate icing.

Date Squares

1 lb. dates
1 cup of water
1/2 cup granulated sugar
Cook until thick, let cool.

Filling

1/2 cup butter
1 cup brown sugar
1 cup flour and 1 tsp. soda
2 1/2 cups rolled oats.
Mix until all fine and crumbly. Spread one-half of mixture in pan, put filling on top of mixture, then remainder of mixture. Bake until brown.

Kate Maxner.

Peanut Butter Balls

1 cup confectionery sugar
1 cup peanut butter
        pinch salt
½ cup chopped nuts
¼ cup chopped dates

Roll in balls and dip in thin confectionery sugar (icing). Roll in cocoanut.

Viola E. Smith
Mrs. R.C.

Mocha Cakes

1 hot milk cake cut in small squares

Dip in thin icing made from:
    1 cup confectioner's sugar
    Strong coffee and vanilla
    Roll in chopped peanuts

Viola E. Smith.
(Mrs. R.C.)

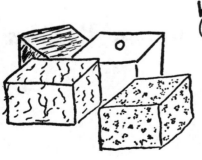

287

BROWNIES

1 cup sugar
½ cup butter
2 eggs
1 cup pastry flour
½ cup walnuts
2 sq. melted chocolate
vanilla

Cream butter, add sugar and well beaten eggs. Then nuts, chocolate, flour and vanilla. Bake about 12 min. at 400°. Put frosting on brownies as soon as they are taken from the oven.

Vivian P. Zinck
(Mrs. R.C.)

Yum Yums

YUM!
YUM!

½ cup butter
1 cup brown sugar
1 egg
1 cup sour milk
1 tsp. soda, sifted with
2 cups pastry flour
1 tsp cinnamon, cloves
and nutmeg.
¼ tsp. salt
1 cup chopped walnuts
1 cup cut dates.

Cream butter and sugar, add egg (unbeaten) beat well. Add soda and spices
to sifted, measured flour, sift and add
alternately with sour milk. Add dates
and nuts. Bake in cupcake tins in
oven, 350° temp. Good with coffee or
brown sugar fudge icing —

Georgie M. Mason (Mrs. H.F.)
289

⟵ DREAMS ⟶

Whites of 3 eggs beaten stiffly
   1 c. white sugar. add gradually
Stir on stove over hot water until
it crusts on sides and bottom of
saucepan. Take from heat
    Add —
        1 tbsp. Cornstarch
        1 c. Nuts
        1 c. dates
        1 c. Cocoanut
Drop on buttered pan. Bake a few
minutes in moderate oven. While warm
Remove carefully with spatula

Dorothy E. Geldart
(Mrs. L. W.)

Almond Strips

5 eggs.
¾ cup white sugar.
½ lb. almonds - put through
chopper - skins and all.
vanilla and salt.

Separate eggs. To well beaten
yolks add sugar and beat well.
Add almonds, vanilla and salt
to well beaten whites and
combine the two mixtures.
Bake in a 9 by 12 from 35 to
40 mins ... 350° oven. When cool
frost with a butter icing
tinted a very pale green.

Mrs. Phil. Bachman.

Lemon Slices

½ C. Butter creamed with ½ C. white sugar
Roll out about 15 graham wafers fine. Take out
1 Cup of them add to butter & sugar mixture. Bake
in pan 8 x 8 in mod. oven for 15 mins.

Filling :—

1 lemon - juice & rind
3 tsp. water
3 egg yolks   ¾ C. sugar
3 egg whites   ⅓ C. flour

Mix sugar & flour, add lemon juice, rind
and warm water. Beat thoroughly then add
beaten egg yolks slowly, beating mixture all
the time. Cook over boiling water until
thick stirring constantly. Then fold in
beaten egg whites. Pour over first
mixture & sprinkle with remaining crumbs.
Bake 15-20 mins. in moderate oven.

Catharine M. Creighton (Mrs. H. A)

292

Almond Bars.

½ cup butter
⅓ cup sugar
3 egg yolks
rind of 1 orange
    or lemon
2 tbsp. milk
1½ cups flour
1 tsp. Baking Powder.

Line a large buttered
pan with mixture and
spread on top —
3 egg whites beaten
stiff and dry
        add
½ cup sugar
½ cup chopped
blanched almonds
1 tsp. almond flavoring.
    Bake 15 or 20 minutes
in oven 350°.
        Audrey M. Smith
    293   (Mrs. W. W.)

Mystery Cakes

½ cup soft butter
½ cup brown sugar
2 cups sifted pastry flour
Cream butter and sugar, add flour
Blend together and turn into 9 or 10
inch cake tin. Pat evenly.
Combine 1½ cups brown sugar, 2 tbsps.
flour, 1½ tsps. baking powder
1½ tsps salt, 2 eggs, 1 cup chopped dates
½ cup cocoanut, 1 cup chopped walnuts.
Spread on top of first mixture in
pan. Bake 40 minutes in a
moderate oven. When cool frost
with butter icing. Cut in size
desired.

Marian D. Zwicker
(Mrs. F. Homer)

294

Orange Squares.

1 tbsp. Shortening or Butter

½ cup Sugar.

2 Eggs.

2/3 cup. Orange Marmalade

1 cup Bran Flakes

2/3 cup. Flour.

1 tsp. Salt.

1 tsp. Baking Powder.

½ cup. Chopped Nuts

Cream shortening and sugar Add eggs, marmalade and bran flakes. Mix well. Add dry ingredients and nuts. Pour into 8" (greased) pan. Bake 30 min. in 375° oven

Alice J. Burke
(Mrs. Dougald)

295

Cheese Triangles

½ Cup butter
¼ lb. cream cheese
1 tablespoon brown sugar
1½ cups flour
½ teaspoon baking powder

Crumble this mixture, pat half
on pan, cover with jelly, then
rest of mixture, bake in mod.
oven 30 min. cut when cool.

Maud Morrow Bailly
(Mrs. L. D.)

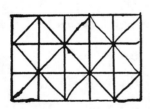

Cheese Creams

¼ lb. creamed cheese

¼ lb. butter

1 cup flour

Cream well together.
Roll thin, cut with
cookie cutter, put
together with jelly.
Bake in oven 375°

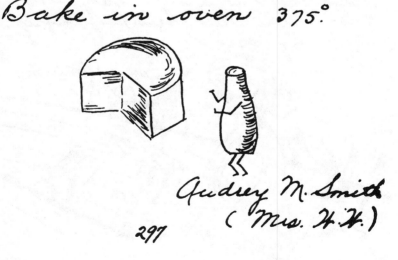

297

Audrey M. Smith
(Mrs. H.H.)

Queen of the Sea Cookies

First layer:
  ½ cup butter (cream)
Add 2½ cups rolled graham wafers.
Pack in pans. Bake at 325° for 15 minutes
Second layer.
  ½ cup butter   ⎤ cream
  1½ cups icing sugar.⎦ together
Add 2 egg yolks unbeaten.
Spread on first layer.
Third layer.
  ½ pint cream whipped.
  add 1 can crushed pineapple (drained)
  Add 3 tbls sugar.
Spread on second layer. Freeze for
2 hours. Cut while frozen. Keep in frig.
Makes 2 pans 8" by 4"

Gracie Walters.
(Mrs. B. J.)

298

Calla Lilies

½ cup potato flour (good)
4 eggs
½ teaspoon baking powder
Pinch of salt
1 cup sugar (small)
Beat eggs well.

Add sugar, beat again, then add flour and baking powder. Bake in round pans 4 inch ungreased, a delicate brown. Remove from pans and fold to form a lily. Put a toothpick to hold together. Fill with whipped cream, flavoured with sugar and vanilla. Add a strip of orange jello.

Maple Anderson

299

Rocky Mountain Peaks.

Beat 2 eggs well, add 1 cup icing sugar and while hot, 4 squares Chocolate (unsweetened) which have been melted with one tsp. butter. Add 1 cup chopped walnuts and 20 marshmallows, cut into pieces Drop on wax paper and allow to stand for a couple of hours.

Elizabeth Winters
(Mrs. C.A.)

300

Meringues

Whites of three eggs beaten stiff until you can turn bowl upside down. Add one cup of sugar and pinch of salt and beat until it holds its shape.

Drop by tablespoon on a hardwood board which has been wet with cold water, place wax paper on board. Bake in slow oven about 2 hours, they should dry out, when dry and firm remove from oven and scoop out any portion not hardened. Put back in oven until dry.

Rosa Iversen
(Mrs P. K.)

Doughnuts

2 eggs
1 cup sugar
3 tbsp. melted butter
1 cup milk
7 tsp. baking powder
1/4 tsp. salt
1/4 flavoring.

Mix in order given.
Add all purpose flour
to make a soft dough
cut out and fry in hot
lard.

Marion Sterne

Ralston Chocolate Caramels

3 cups sugar ¼ lb. chocolate
⅓ cup milk ¼ lb. butter
⅓ cup water 1 tsp. vanilla
⅔ cup molasses, pinch of salt
¼ or ½ lb. blanched almonds

Put first four ingredients on to boil. Stir until sugar is melted. Then add chocolate. Stir until it is melted. Then add butter, but do not stir. Put the toasted and cut up almonds into a buttered pan. When the candy cracks in cold water, pour it over the nuts, but don't put in the scrapings. Cut in squares.

A Picnic at the Ovens Park.

Minnie C. Hewitt

Sugar Candy

2 cups sugar

½ cup vinegar

1 tsp butter

Boil until candy brittles when dropped in cold water. Pour on buttered plates to cool. Pull to a nice light color. Cut desired size and wrap in wax paper.

Hazel Allen
(Mrs. Robert)

Molasses Candy

1 cup molasses
1½ cups sugar
½ cup water
⅛ tsp soda

1½ tbsp. vinegar
¼ tsp. cream of tartar
4 tbsp. melted butter

Cook molasses, sugar, water and vinegar in heavy pan, stirring constantly. When boiling point is reached, add cream of tartar. Boil until mixture is brittle when tried in cold water (256°F). Stir constantly during last part of cooking. When nearly done, add butter and soda. Turn on buttered shallow pan and when cool, pull until porous and light colored. While pulling add 1 tsp. vanilla or few drops oil of peppermint. Cut in small pieces and wrap in wax paper, or cut in shape the size of suckers, and put on sticks before candy becomes hard. You may use balloon sticks, cut in size desired. These are always enjoyed by the young folk

Joyce L. Tupper (Mrs. J. A.)

306

Chocolate Fudge.

3 cups white sugar.
1 c. brown sugar
4 large Tbsp. Tbsp cocoa.
1 c. milk, $\frac{1}{8}$ tsp. cream of tartar
pinch of salt, 1 Tbsp. butter
1 tsp vanilla, cut walnuts.
Combine all ingredients except
butter, vanilla and nuts in a heavy
aluminum sauce pan. Keep
stirring on low heat until
thoroughly dissolved, increase heat and boil,
stirring frequently, until it collects and forms
a soft ball, when tried in cold water. Remove
from stove, add butter and vanilla, Set aside
until partly cool, then beat until creamy, add
nuts and pour in pan. mark in squares for cutting.

OH BOY
FUDGE!

Brown Sugar Fudge.

3 c. brown sugar
1 c. white sugar
3 c. milk, $\frac{1}{8}$ tsp c. of tartar
pinch salt, tsp vanilla
1 Tbsp. butter. nuts.

White Cocoanut Fudge

4 cups white sugar
1 c. milk, $\frac{1}{8}$ tsp c. of t.
pinch salt, tsp vanilla
1 Tbsp. butter, 1 c.
fine shredded
cocoanut.

Same method as above. As a variation of
brown sugar Fudge, omit vanilla and nuts and
add $\frac{1}{2}$ c. peanut butter as well as butter when removed from stove. Add cocoanut to white fudge
just before pouring in pan.

Georgie M. Mason
(Mrs Harold).

309

Divinity Fudge

2 cups white sugar
½ cup corn syrup
½ cup cold water
2 stiffly beaten egg whites
½ cup chopped walnuts
1 tsp. vanilla

Boil sugar, corn syrup, water without stirring for 10 minutes after it has started to boil hard. Take one cup of this syrup and pour slowly over stiffly beaten egg whites. Put remainder of syrup back on stove and after it starts to boil again, boil 5 minutes longer. Keep beating egg mixture until all the syrup has been used up. Add vanilla and nuts. Beat until stiff. Pour into greased pan and when cool cut in squares.

Muriel E. Hebb.
(Mrs. E. H.)

FONDANT FOR PEPPERMINT PATTIES

8 tbs. Corn Syrup, 4 tbs. soft Butter, 3 lbs. sifted Icing Sugar, 1 can Condensed Milk. Add peppermint flavoring to taste.

Mix well until it kneads like heavy dough. Roll dough to 1/8 inch thick. Use small cookie cutter for cutting patties. Let harden on wax paper, then dip.
(Dough may be divided into portions for various flavors and colors.)

FONDANT FOR MARASCHINO CHERRIES

1 egg white beaten stiff, 1 lb. sifted Icing sugar, 1 bottle Maraschino Cherries, 3/4 tsp. almond flavoring. Add icing sugar gradually to egg white and flavoring until a soft ball can be rolled. Drain Cherries well. Cover each cherry with the fondant. Set on wax paper for 2 hours. Then dip in chocolate..

CHOCOLATE DIPPING

(Unsweetened Choc. may be used for patties. Semi-sweet choc. may be used for other chocolates such as Cherries, Nuts, Raisins etc.)

1/2 lb. bar of Chocolate (Sweetened or Unsweetened.), 1/2 cake paraffin wax. Melt in tall can over boiling water, cool slightly and then dip fondant or nuts on a spoon. Let cool on wax paper.

FRANCES FRITTENBURG
(MRS. M. W.)

309

Potato Candy.

Boil a medium size potato and mash while hot.

Work in with a spoon, 1 lb pulverized sugar, 1 c cocoanut, and vanilla.

Press into a buttered pan and pour 2 sq. slightly cooled unsweetened chocolate over top, or omit chocolate and spread topping on.

Topping

3 tsp Cocoa
1 c pulverized sugar
Mix with a little hot water to make soft.
Spread on top of candy and sprinkle with cocoanut.

Beulah Thurlow.
(Mrs James)

310

Pickles
AND
Preserves

311

= CHOW. CHOW =

1. pk. tomatoes,
6. large onions,
cut tomatoes, add ½ cup salt,
let stand over night, next day
drain thoroughly, then place a
layer of tomatoes and onions in
kettle, add 3 teaspoons mustard,
½ tsp. tumeric, 1 cup sugar,
Repeat this until 4 cups sugar is
used, add 1 qt. vinegar, + ½ cup
water, 2 tsps whole pickling
spice in piece of cheese cloth, cook
until tomatoes + onions are quite soft.

L. M. Beginn.
(m rs Foster)

312

Bread and Butter Pickles

6 qts. sliced medium cucumbers.

1½ qts. vinegar.

6 cups sugar.

6 onions medium size sliced.

1 cup salt.

½ cup mustard. seed.

1 tbsp. celery seed.

¼ to ⅓ tsp. Cayenne pepper.

Combine cucumbers, onions, and salt, let stand three hours. Drain, Combine seasoning and vinegar, and boil.

Add cucumbers, and onions. Heat to simmering, and pack hot. Be careful to avoid boiling as that makes pickles soft. Pack while hot in clean jars and seal immediately.

Flo .E. Powers.
(Mrs. A.F.)

Nine Day Pickles

5 qts. Cucumbers; quarter and cut in lengths about one inch long,

2 large Cauliflowers; broken into flowerets,

2 lb. Silver Skin Onions (whole)

Put in crock with 1 cup Salt dissolved in 2 qts. Boiling Water. Cool and pour over Cukes, etc. and let stand 3 days. Drain brine off, scalding same and pour over pickles and repeat three days. Rinse well — let cold water pour over them. Then take 1 gallon Boiling Water in which 1 tbsp. Alum is dissolved and pour over and let stand 6 hours. Drain and rinse well under running water and make the following syrup :—

1½ qts. Vinegar

1 oz. Cinnamon Stick

1 cup Water

4 lb. White Sugar (if you like sweet Pickles add another pound Sugar)

1 oz Mustard Seed } Put in cheesecloth bag.
1 oz Allspice Berries }

Pour over Cukes and add, if desired, sweet red peppers for color.

These can be stored in the crock.

Hazel Smith Geldert
314 (Mrs. E. C.)

Mustard Pickles

1 quart of ripe cucumbers
or cauliflower
1 qt. chopped celery.
1 qt. onions.
2 sweet green peppers.
2 sweet red peppers.

Scald for 10 minutes in one quart
of white vinegar.

Add - 3 cups white sugar.
1 tsp. tumeric.
3 tsp. mustard.
3/4 cup. flour.
1 tbsp. salt.
2 tsp. mustard seed.

Blend with a little cold
vinegar, stirring until thick
Bring to a boil. Then
bottle at once.

(Mrs. W. P.) Mildred G. Potter

315

Dutch Salad

2 Quarts Cucumbers
1 Quart Cauliflower
1 Quart Onions
1 Quart Green Tomatoes
1 Quart Celery
3 Red Sweet Peppers

Chop fine and cover with Brine
(8 qts. boiling water and 1 Pint Salt —
cool before pouring over vegetables)
Let stand over night — heat enough
to scald, then drain thoroughly
Make a paste of the following: —
1 Tbsp. Tumeric
1 heaping cup Flour
10 Tbsp. Dry Mustard
add 2 quarts Vinegar and 7 cups
granulated sugar
Boil this until it thickens and
is smooth, stirring all the time
then add vegetables and cook gently
until heated well

Hazel Smith Geldert
(Mrs. E.C.)

316

East Indian Pickle

3 qts. green tomatoes
3 qts. ripe tomatoes
1 qt. onions
1 bunch celery
4 peppers
½ cup salt
 Cover with plate and
  let stand overnight,
1 tbls. cloves
1 tbls. cinnamon
¼ cup mustard seed
1½ lbs. sugar
1¾ qts. vinegar
 Boil until done,

Sadie A. Krickee
(Mrs J. R.)

Cucumber Relish

12 or 14 large cucumbers, peeled
seeded and diced.
4 cups onions, chopped fine
½ cup salt.
Combine and let stand overnight. Put dish on to heat
in the morning. When heated,
drain and add to the
following mixture, which
has been cooked.

1 qt. vinegar	1 tsp. celery seed
5 c. sugar	1 " mustard seed
1 c. flour	1 " turmeric

Boil all together for 10 min.,
then bottle

Pickled Beets

4 cups sliced cold cooked beets
2 cups vinegar
⅓ cup sugar
½ tsp. salt
1 tbsp. mixed whole pickling
   spice tied in cheesecloth.
Put beets in clean hot jars,
cover with hot spiced vinegar
and seal.

Ethie Hamm
(Mrs. J. H.)

318

Pickled Watermelon Rind

Four lbs of rind - 2 lbs of granulated sugar. 3/4 pint of vinegar. Prepare and peel and cut watermelon rind into strips about 1 inch wide - 2 inches long. Boil vinegar and sugar for 15 minutes. Add rind and cook until Tender, Bottle and seal.

Mrs. Cronin
(Thos W. B)

319

RHUBARB RELISH

[GOOD WITH FISH]

2 quarts cut rhubarb

2 quarts onions – scald
and throw water away

1 cups white sugar

3 cups cider vinegar

2 tsp. salt

1 tsp pepper

2 Tsp ground cloves

2 tsp. cinnamon

Cook thoroughly until quite thick

Josephine Eisenhower

(Mrs. D. A.)

Chili Sauce.

30 ripe tomatoes (peeled)
10 small onions (chopped)
6 green peppers
16 tbsp. sugar
5 tbsp. salt (scant)
1 pt. vinegar.
Boil 1½ hours.

Alice Adams.
(Mrs. E. C.)

Tomato Marmalade.

4 lbs. ripe tomatoes.
4 oranges.
1 lemon.
4 lbs. white sugar.
Skin tomatoes, slice oranges and lemons, including rind. Let boil 5 min. Add sugar and boil until it jells.

Alice Adams.
(Mrs. E. C.)

Golden Marmalade

Slice 6 oranges and 3 lemons very fine discarding seeds. Cover the sliced fruit with water and let stand overnight. Next morning boil the fruit and water mixture 45 minutes. Let stand overnight again.

In the morning measure and then bring to a boil. Add 1½ times as much sugar as fruit. Boil 45 minutes. Just before the marmalade is removed from the heat add 1 cup of lemon juice. Seal in glasses. The resulting marmalade is tart and distinctive in flavour, but not at all bitter, and the color is clear and golden.

Edythe E. Oxner
(Mrs. J. W.)

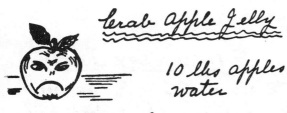

Crab Apple Jelly

10 lbs apples   sugar
water   salt

Wash apples. Remove stems and blossoms, cut in small pieces. Cover apples with water and boil 2 hours. Mash with potato masher and put in bag. Drain overnight. Measure juice in large pot and let come to a rolling boil. Heat equal amount of sugar, plus 1 cup for the pot. Add to boiling juice and boil hard 20 minutes. Pour at once in sterilized jars. Delicious with roast chicken. If spiced jelly preferred. Tie 2 oz. mixed pickling spice in cloth and boil in jelly.

———— '' ————

Peach Conserve

12 peaches — peeled, stoned and mashed
6 oranges — put thru food chopper
3 lbs sugar

Combine all ingredients and boil like marmalade. About 1 hr.

Lois J. Himmelman
(Mrs Thomas)

323

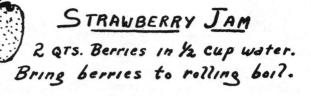

STRAWBERRY JAM

2 QTS. Berries in ½ cup water.
Bring berries to rolling boil.

Add 2 cups Sugar. Bring to rolling boil. Boil
hard for 3 MIN.
Add 2 more cups Sugar. Bring to rolling
boil. Boil 3 MIN.
Add 2 more cups Sugar. Bring to rolling
boil for 3 MIN.
Pour into sterilized Jars.

Frances Frittenburg
(Mrs. M.W.)

PRESSURE CANNING of RASPBERRIES

Wash carefully. Drain. Fill pint jars
with raw berries and shake down
for full pack to ½ inch from top
of Jar. Cover with boiling thin
syrup (1 cup Sugar to 2 cups water).
Adjust lids. Process 8 min. with
stem at 5 lbs. Pressure.

Frances Frittenburg
(Mrs. M.W.)

SPICED GOOSEBERRIES

4   qts. berries
3½   lbs. sugar
1   pt. vinegar (scant)
1   tbsp. each of cloves,
     cinnamon and mixed spice
(or all spice in place of mixed spice)

Place ingredients in kettle. Mix well.
Boil over medium heat until thickened—
about 1-1½ hrs. Stir frequently. Pour
in sterilized jars and seal. Very tasty
with roast beef or cold cuts.

Evelyn V. Zinck
(Mrs. B. E.)

325

Mince Meat

5 Cups chopped cooked beef or venson (2½ lbs)
2½ Cups chopped suet   (1 lb.)
   7½ Cups chopped apples
   3 Cups apple cider or apple juice
   ½ Cup vinegar, 3/4 lb. citron
   1 Cup molasses
   5 Cups white sugar
   2½ Cups whole raisins (cut fine)
   1½ Cups raisins
      1½ Tbsp salt
juice of 2 lemons or 2 oranges
      1 Tbsp mace
2 scant   { cinnamon
Tbsp each   { cloves
             { allspice

   2 nutmegs grated, 1 tsp almond
   2 Tbsp. lemon extract, 1½ Cups Brandy
   3 Cups liquid in which beef was cooked.
Mix ingredients in order given. Let simmer
1½ hours. Add brandy and shavings from
rind of lemons and oranges.
   Bottle or put in large earthern crock.

               Catharine M. Creighton (Mrs. H.A.)

                      326

MEN'S
dishes

GENIUS
AT WORK

327

BACKMAN

RUM PUNCH

One of Sour
Two of Sweet
Three of Strong
And Four of Weak

1 ounce Sour, 2 ounces Sweet, 3 ounces Strong, 4 ounces Weak makes 10 ounces of Punch, about enough for three drinks. Use any multiple of the above proportions for the number you want to serve.

Sour – preferably the juice of fresh limes
    or lemon juice, fresh or canned
Sweet – simple syrup (equal parts of sugar
    and water, boiled for five minutes)
Strong – preferably Barbados rum,
    though any rum can be used
Weak – combined water and ice

Pour the 3 parts of rum into any mixing bowl or container, add the 1 part of Sour, stirring well, then add 2 parts of Sweet and continue the stirring until thoroughly mixed (about 15 minutes).

This mixture can be made and bottled in advance and added to the 4 parts of water and ice just before serving, at which time the cut-up skins of citrus fruit can be added to enhance the flavour.

When serving, add a dash or two of Angostura Bitters to the top of each glass. A sprinkle of nutmeg can also be used, if desired.

F. Homer Zwicker

Seafood Cocktail

Measure.

2 teaspoons prepared Horseradish.
3 tablespoons tomato catsup or chili sauce
1 teaspoon salt.
2 tablespoons vinegar.
4 tablespoons lemon juice.
¼ teaspoon tabasco sauce.
1 teaspoon grated onion

Method.

Mix all ingredients, making a sauce.
Place lettuce leaf in chilled cocktail glass,
add seafood and cover with sauce.

Note.

Raw oysters, lobster, shrimp, fried clams
or fried scallops can be used as
seafood for this cocktail.

John Carne.
(chef - Boscumentram)

329

Oyster Stew

3 doz. oysters
4 tbsps. butter

1 qt. Milk
Salt, pepper

Drain oysters well; save juice.
Put one tbsp. butter in frying pan.
— add oysters; cook until edges curl.
Heat juice separately.
Add butter, oysters and juice to
scalded milk. Season to taste.
Let stand to blend before serving.
Serves six.

Clam Chowder

1 pt. fresh clams
1 qt. milk
4 average-size potatoes

1 onion
4 tbsps butter
salt
pepper

Peel and dice potatoes — cover
with cold water; add salt
— cook with finely chopped onion
until tender.
Cook clams in their own juice.
Scald milk.
Combine all ingredients —
adding salt, pepper and butter.

Bluenose Lodge
Fred. A. Slakk.

Curling Club Favourites
POT ROAST >

4 lb. Rump or Rib roast (cut thick)

Put in pot with little shortening, pepper + salt
to taste. 1 onion, 2 carrots peeled + split, few
pieces celery. Dredge with flour, not too heavy.
Add about 1 cup water in bottom of pot.

Simmer on stove until done. (about 4 hrs.)

FISH CHOWDER

6 potatoes (diced)

1 small onion (chopped fine)

pinch of pepper + salt

Put on to boil, cook partly done.
Add: 1½ lb. haddock fillet, cook until done.
"   1½ pt. milk. (Take off stove before adding
milk). Put ½ can evaporated milk, ¼ lb. butter, 1 tsp.
sugar. Pepper + salt to tast. Let come to a
boil (but Not Boil).

W. Guy Tanner

To Boil Lobsters

For 10 lbs. Lobsters
Take 1 gal. water and
2 tbsp. salt. When
water comes to hard
boil put in lobsters.
Boil for 20 min. or until
legs and small claws
pull free from body.
Serve hot dipped in
vinegar and melted
butter or mayonnaise or
cold in salads, fish
cocktails. etc.

332 Aubrey A. Levy.

Baked Live Lobster

To Split a Live Lobster

Cross large claws and hold firmly with left hand. With a sharp knife, held in right hand, begin at the mouth and make a deep incision, with a sharp cut, draw the knife quickly through body and entire length of tail. Open lobster and remove intestinal vein, liver and stomach. Crack claws by giving each a good wallop with a hammer.

Place lobster in baking dish, shell side down.

Mix — 1 cup bread crumbs — 3 tbsp melted butter
1 tbsp lemon juice. — dash of salt and cayenne
With liver of Lobster

Fill cavities in lobster with mixture. Bake in oven 375°F for 30 to 40 minutes depending on size of lobster. Baste twice during baking with melted butter and again before taking from oven

Lobster Mu Guy

Take meat from 2 medium sized boiled lobsters, when cold chop coarse. Put in frying pan, 3 oz. butter {4 egg-sized onion, 1 clove garlic) chopped fine, 2 sticks celery, (diced, let fry until done, but not brown. Add lobster meat, pinch nutmeg, ⅓ tsp. salt, pinch of pepper, ½ tsp. sugar, 2 tbsp. tomato ketchup, 1 tsp. worcestershire sauce, pinch of horseradish, pinch of paprika, few drops of tabasco sauce, ½ tbsp. flour.

Let simmer 25 min, then add 2 tbsp. grated cheese, let cook 10 min.

A delicious dish served on toast or in patty shells.

P.S. — 4 chopped mushrooms can be added to the above receipe.

W. Guy Tanner

334

FRYING TROUT

To fry pan size trout,
clean fish, cut off head and
tail, sprinkle with salt;
roll in flour and fry
in plenty of butter.

I like trout fried whole
but those who prefer to fry
them crisp -- split the fish,
treat as above and
fry. For added taste serve with
"Fiddlehead" Greens.

F. J. Bourque

Broiled Salmon
(Outdoors)

A three to seven pound salmon is ideal for broiling on an open fire. Split the fish through the back from head to tail. Remove head and back bone. Place the fish skin side down on a hard wood plank, or split log a few inches longer and wider than the fish. (An open fire toaster may be used.) Secure with skewers and place strips of bacon or salt pork about two inches apart over the fish. Then stand before an open fire. Allow about ten minutes for each inch of thickness of fish.

(Indoors)

Prepare fish in the same manner. A large fish may be used, as the fish is cut crosswise in three inch strips. Place strip of bacon on each piece of fish. Place on a tray seven inches below pre-heated broiler. Thick fish may be turned to insure thorough cooking

J. A. MacDuff

338

Salmon Omlettes

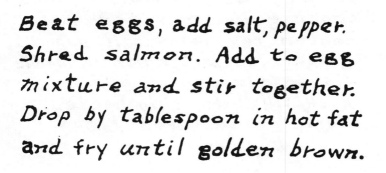

1b. can of salmon
4 or 5 eggs
Salt, pepper

Beat eggs, add salt, pepper.
Shred salmon. Add to egg
mixture and stir together.
Drop by tablespoon in hot fat
and fry until golden brown.

Roy Whynacht

Creamed Chicken Haddie (canned

1 can Chicken Haddie
2 Egg Yolks
1 cup Ginger Ale
3 tbsp. Butter
3 " Flour
¾ cup Milk or Cream

Make cream sauce by melting
butter, adding flour, milk and
cooking five minutes. Add
beaten egg yolks, salt, paprika,
ginger ale and chicken haddie,
flaked fine.
Cook till thoroughly heated.
Serve on buttered toast.

Roy Whynacht

338

Fish in Batter.

Measure

2 cups sifted flour
2 teaspoons salt
2 teaspoons sugar
2 well beaten eggs
1 cup cold milk

Method

Mix all ingredients, add well beaten eggs,
add cup of cold milk.
Cut fish in two inch squares.
Fry in deep fat at temp. 350 - 360 degrees
F. until brown.
Serve with Tomato or Chili Sauce.

Note.

Frozen fish should be thawed and dried
before dipping in batter.

John Corner.
(chef - Boscowan Menu)

339

Steamed Clams
Done in seaweed on Out-door Fireplace

Build fireplace with stones on beach, prepare fire. Place a large piece of tin or an "oven grate" about one foot from base of fire. Put a layer of seaweed on top of grate and then clams, alternating with clams and seaweed. Leave clams on fire for 10 mins.

Boiled Green Corn
Done on Out-door Fireplace

Prepare fire-place as above.
A large container

The husks should be left on until just before the corn is to be boiled.

Plunge the husked ears into the boiling water and cook for 12 to 15 mins. Do not salt the cooking water, as this toughens the corn.

Art. Bailly

340

YOUR OWN FINNAN HADDIE

Get up at 4 A.M. to catch and cure haddock the same day. Treat the gulls to the heads and internals while still at sea. Immediately on landing split and wash haddock. Then immerse in pickle (strong enough to float a potato) about one hour, more or less, depending on size of fish. After hanging them on rods to dry, you may lunch and catch up in your rest.

Fish should be ready for smoking by dusk. If you must improvise a smoke house, two barrels without heads will suffice. Stand one over a pan of smouldering dry hardwood sawdust and the other one on top of it with the rods of haddock hanging across the top. Cover the top but leave some small openings at bottom and top for draft to keep sawdust smouldering all night.

If you are an enthusiast you will make several trips to the smoke house during the night to check smoke and replenish sawdust if necessary. By breakfast time fish should be ready to eat.

Try broiling about ten minutes in a covered pan with a little water and a dash of nutmeg.

Serve with buttered toast.

Roy Whynacht

343

Duck Stew

Clean two Sea Ducks and
put an onion in each.
Parboil until tender.
Then strip meat from bones.
Put meat in saucepan.
Cover with water and
season with salt and
pepper. Simmer about
one half hour. Thicken
with browned flour.
Add onion if desired.
Serve with boiled potatoes.

W. T. Powers.

Fried Partridge

1 partridge
1/4 cup flour
1 teaspoon salt
1/4 teaspoon pepper
4 tablespoons butter or 2 tablespoons butter & 2 tablespoons
shortening.

    Clean bird and cut
in pieces. Dredge in flour and
sprinkle with salt & pepper. Fry
in hot pan until golden brown.
Lower heat, cover tightly and let
steam until tender. Serve on
hot platter, or with gravy made
of one tablespoon flour added
to fat in pan, then add one
cup of milk and cook until thick.

Mildred Stearns

343

— Venison —

Your appetite has already been whetted by
this superb delicacy – deer liver, sliced,
scalded, dredged in flour salt and pepper &
lightly fried in bacon fat. The stuffed heart
done 45 min. in your pressure cooker has
been a treat and the grilled kidneys have
lifted breakfast out of the ordinary. So now you
are awaiting tenderness and fine flavour
to develop in the meat during 7-14 days
hanging in a dry cold atmosphere (or perhaps
in your refrigerator with the aid of black
pepper and dried herbs – no salt) The haunch
(hind quarter less loin & hock) is the prime
roast; also to provide steaks through the
upper round or rump. The shoulder roast
is good. The saddle (loin and lower ribs) is
a choice roast or may be cut into chops
which should be grilled. Other parts are best
reserved for stewing, braising, venison pies,
or for currying. (waste nothing). The breast is
more esteemed but more important is it
that the beast should have been
quickly killed and well bled. Plenty of creamy
fat is an indication of quality (although
lean meat is characteristic.) Whatever type
of cooking is used be careful to conserve
moisture because this noble meat is dry
in nature and its flavour delicate. A
preliminary marinating before roasting is often
carried out larding, with a special needle
is an improvement. (if you know the art.)

To marinate: 1 large onion (chopped), 2
large carrots (chopped, 3 whole cloves, 1 tsp.
your favourite herbs, 1/2 tsp. black pepper,
4 tbsp. butter & 1 cup cider vinegar (no salt)
Sauté vegetables in butter, add vinegar &
seasonings, pour hot over meat. Turn meat
every 2 hours for 8 hours. (cont. next page)

<u>To Roast</u>: (a) After marinating roast in a covered roaster, with marinade, at 325° (about 25 min per lb.). Baste very frequently.

or (b) After marinating, remove, rub with bacon fat or lard and wrap in a greased paper (not waxed). Tie. Make a stiff paste of flour + water + cover overall. Wrap again in greased paper + tie. Roast at 325° (30 min per lb.) Half an hour before serving remove wrappings, sprinkle lightly with flour and salt and brown in a hot oven.

<u>To Grill Steak</u>: Cut steak 1 inch or more thick. Cover top side 1/4 inch deep with medium salt (not shaker salt). Pat smooth + slip under broiler for normal time. Salt will be brown and hard. Turn and repeat salt layer and grilling on other side until done. Then crack off salt shells from each side. Serve all venison on very hot plates — pewter if you have them. (Deer fat while of excellent flavour hardens rapidly (try with beef.)

<u>Accompaniments</u>: Serve red currant (or black) jelly (no pickles or catsup, please). Potatoes should be only baked or boiled in their jackets. To add the finishing touch try the following old English wine sauce which is superb with all game.

Melt a cup of red currant (or black) jelly, add one cup of claret, bring to simmer + add a pinch of powdered ginger, a pinch of ground cloves, allspice and 1 tbsp. of lemon juice. Add an equal part of strained game gravy (no fat), and sufficient flour to thicken. As an exotic variant add 1 tbsp of brandy or sherry before serving.

This meat of Kings is our heritage from the wild. Never for sale, its preparation must ever remain a home art. To borrow from Dr. Johnson let it not be said that it was ill-killed, ill-prepared, ill-cooked and ill-served.

345   — Arthur James —.

Baked Beans

3 cups beans
½ lb. fresh pork
2 medium onions
1 tsp. dry mustard
1 tbsp. salt
½ tsp. pepper
½ cup sugar o⁄ molasses

Wash beans and soak overnight. Next morning add ingredients. Cover with water. Stir occasionally. Bake for 2½ hours in electric stove at 350° F. In cook stove 7-8 hrs. at 300° F.

Clarence W. Allen.
346

Election Cake.

"Everybody Vote"

Five pounds of sifted flour, rubbed with 2 pounds of butter; 2 pounds of sugar; 1½ pints of home made yeast, 2 pounds raisins, 8 tablespoonfuls of wine, 8 tablespoonfuls of brandy; 4 Eggs, 1 quart of sweet milk, 2 pounds currents, 1 pound of citron, half ounce of grated nutmeg. To the butter and flour add half the sugar; then the yeast and half the milk. Lukewarm in summer; hot in winter. Beat well and let rise in a warm place all night. In the morning beat some time, adding the brandy, sugar, spice and fruit (well floured) and let rise again very light. After which put in cake pans, and let rise 10 or 15 minutes. Have the oven about as hot as for bread. Temperance people can use 2 extra eggs and 2 wine glasses of rose water to take the place of the liquor with as good, if not better results.

Geo. P. Corkum

Dear Reader.
   This book was compiled
For your culinery pleasure.
We hope you will find it
   A veritable treasure.

If to you it becomes
A friend tried and true
We'll be glad that our efforts
Brought it to you

The Ladies Auxiliary
of the
Lunenburg Hospital Society